BASQUE FOR ENGLISH SPEAKERS

BASQUE FOR
ENGLISH SPEAKERS

BEATRIZ FERNÁNDEZ

English translation and adaptation for
English-speaking readers by
Eider Etxebarria Zuluaga

N

CENTER FOR BASQUE STUDIES
UNIVERSITY OF NEVADA, RENO
2021

This book was published with generous financial support from the Basque Government.

Center for Basque Studies
University of Nevada, Reno
1664 North Virginia St,
Reno, Nevada 89557 usa
http://basque.unr.edu

English translation and adaptation for English-speaking readers by
    Eider Etxebarria Zuluaga.

Cover Design by Rebecca Lown

LIBRARY OF CONGRESS CATALOGING-IN-PUBLICATION DATA

Names: Fernández, Beatriz, author.
Title: Basque for English speakers / Beatriz Fernández.
Description: Reno : Center for Basque Studies, [2021] | Series: Occasional papers
    series ; no. 28 | Summary: "This book aims to introduce English speakers to the
    Basque language. The book also intends to show that two very different languages
    like Basque and English are more similar than might appear at first glance. In fact,
    all human languages are similar to one another in their most essential features, as
    they are particular exponents of one single linguistic faculty. While differences exist
    in particular aspects, English and Basque, when further explored, present more
    similarities than expected"-- Provided by publisher.
Identifiers: LCCN 2021001264 | ISBN 9781949805376 (paperback)
Subjects: LCSH: Basque language--Grammar. | Basque language--Grammar,
    Comparative--English. | English language--Grammar, Comparative--Basque.
Classification: LCC PH5023 .F47 2021 | DDC 499/.9282421--dc23
LC record available at https://lccn.loc.gov/2021001264

Printed in the United States of America

For Heliodora Pedrosa and Antonio Fernández,
who came and stayed.

For María del Carmen Fernández and Edelmiro Fernández,
who gifted me their language and the language of our land.

Contents

Introduction

This book is intended to introduce English-speakers to Basque, a language spoken by about 750,000 inhabitants of the Basque Country and Basque diaspora. Although at first glance Basque and English may seem like very different languages, the reader will find that they are more similar than one would suppose. In fact, both Basque and English are constructions built using the same building blocks. Though the blocks are not assembled in quite the same way in the two languages, they follow the same basic instruction manual.

That said, analyzing languages is not simply a matter of figuring out how to stack blocks. Reflecting on a language and the sentences that we construct from it in some ways resembles the pleasure experienced by a film buff. A verb like *kiss*, for example, brings to mind an event, which in turn leads to thoughts of *who* kissed *whom*—say, Ingrid Bergman and Humphrey Bogart in *Casablanca*. Thus, a verb implies what linguists call two "arguments," like the two characters who interact in a movie scene. In other words, languages are always telling stories, featuring great stars in unforgettable locations and at timeless moments.

On the other hand, one can regard analyzing the nature of a language as something like Sherlock Holmes trying to solve a case: the answer to what at first seems like an unsolvable mystery gradually takes form when we—like Holmes—can open our minds objectively to the (linguistic) evidence, allowing us to make sense out of apparent chaos.

And those who have no interest in building blocks, telling tales, or deciphering conundrums can always just relax and enjoy the linguistic "cuisine" of a foreign culture. Because the fascinating variety we find in the world of gastronomy is not so different from the great variation we find among languages—or even among the different dialects of a single language. It may be true that there is only one Basque linguistic "cuisine," but each Basque dialect (modern Basque has five) and variety "cooks" in its own way using the same primary ingredients afforded by the language.

This book is unique in that it sets out the linguistic features of Basque and compares them to English (as well as other languages) in a way that will be easy for the reader without academic grounding in linguistics to understand. But its focus is not merely limited to the nuts and bolts of language: it also touches on topics related to the culture of Basque-speakers, ranging from cinema and cuisine to the first Basque expedition to scale Mount Everest. After all, as much more than just a tool for communicating information, language is closely bound to the community of speakers' cultural, social, and historical identity.

Though primarily intended for English-speakers, this book will prove useful for speakers of any language who wish to learn about Basque. As noted, familiarity with linguistics as an academic discipline is not a prerequisite. However, the book should also be of interest to anyone curious about the concept of "grammar" in general—what grammar is and how it works, be it in Basque or any other language—since some explanation is provided for topics such as word order, case marking, verbal inflection, and agreement systems, all illustrated by showing how these linguistic phenomena are manifested in Basque in comparison with other languages.

This book consists of seven chapters. Following an introductory general definition of language and grammar in chapter 1, chapters 2 to 5 present the core features of Basque. Specifically, chapter 2 looks at the ways in which Basque and other languages form the unit called a "word" by fusing or agglutinating smaller fragments. Chapter 3 compares how words are ordered into sentences in Basque and English, focusing mainly but not exclusively on the question of whether a verb comes before or after its object. Chapter 4 explains the most salient aspects of verbal inflection in Basque, such as person, gender, and number agreement, as well as auxiliary selection and the distinction between synthetic and analytic forms. One of the most idiosyncratic features of Basque is presented in chapter 5. Finally, while chapter 6 explores the topic of how to create an official "standard" version of a language out of a variety of essentially spoken dialects, chapter 7 looks at precisely the sorts of variation present in the dialects of Basque.

Many people helped bring this project to fruition, and I am deeply indebted to all of them. First, I would like to thank José Ignacio Hualde, Jon Ortiz de Urbina, and two anonymous reviewers for their insightful comments on a previous version of this book. I would also like to acknowledge Michael Stablein, Emily DiFilippo, and Teresa Greppi, who provided me with detailed suggestions on how to improve the quality of the English translation and adaptation of this book. Finally, I am profoundly grateful to those who commented on the original Spanish version of this book, particularly José Antonio Pascual and Juan Carlos Moreno Cabrera, as well as Aritz Arizaga, Maitena Etxebarria, Inazio Mujika, Ane Odria, Antton Olariaga, Anna Pineda, Pello Salaburu, and Koldo Zuazo. As always, all responsibility for oversights or errors remains my own.

Funding for this project was received from the Basque Government (IT1169-19) and the Spanish Ministry of Science and Innovation (PGC2018-096380-B-I00).

1

Lego Blocks and the Manual to Assemble Them

(or how to understand and reflect on languages)

Language is a Lego construction, and grammar is its assembly manual. Grammar is not always about correctness. How we understand and reflect on languages. Basque and English, such distinct languages, so distant, or so similar and close. Isolated languages, related languages. Where are we? Where are we going?

LANGUAGE IS A LEGO CONSTRUCTION, AND GRAMMAR IS ITS ASSEMBLY MANUAL

It is surprisingly difficult to define an everyday tool such as language, and it is even more difficult to explain how it works. Not even the experts agree! The issue at hand is—as with everything else—that the nature of the object is in the eye of the beholder and not in the object itself. I do not pretend to be able to give you here either a unique or a definitive definition of language. Readers do not need it. What I would like to do, instead, is to outline some issues that will probably help readers understand the way researchers in the academic field of linguistics think about language.

While language is inherently universal, many factors are involved in its understanding, including social interactions, cultural proximity, and historical events. Many experts approach the study of languages differently. Here we will focus on the study of language as a human capacity that is exhibited throughout countless languages. There are as many as seven thousand languages on the planet. Some, such as English, Spanish, French, and Mandarin Chinese, have a huge number of speakers, and some others, such as Basque, have considerably fewer speakers. Some languages have an enviable vitality, and others barely scrape by. Some have a solid literary tradition, others a short-lived tradition, and, finally, others do not even have an alphabet. Some are spoken on the slopes of the Himalayas, others in big metropolises; some in exotic and distant islands, others in our neighborhood. Some are official and co-official, such as Spanish and Basque in the Basque Autonomous Community and the Basque-speaking area of Navarre in Spain; others are not, such as Basque in the Basque-speaking area of France, or Asturian, spoken also in an area of Spain, not co-official yet protected. In spite of all these differences, linguists have demonstrated with indisputable arguments that all languages are essentially the same regarding their inner architecture. Here, I am not going to talk about language equality. Rather, I am going to take it for granted that you share this view.

Without getting into convoluted analyses and deep explanations, let's say that language is a Lego set and grammar its assembly manual. This is enough for our purposes. By this I mean that all languages have the same bricks or building blocks, and that even the way of assembling them is amazingly similar, if not almost identical, in all languages. Some grammarians, myself included, even think that the Lego set may be universal; that is, that all human beings possess the same blocks and assemble them in the same ways in constructing language. Grammarians like us strive to explain this universal Lego set and the instructions for assembling it, what we call Universal Grammar. From this perspective, well-assembled Lego blocks are grammatical whereas those that are not well-assembled are ungrammatical.

This ambitious scientific project owes its existence to one of the best-known contemporary American intellectuals, University of Arizona professor Noam Chomsky. The idea that all languages share a common Universal Grammar is, however, considerably older and has forerunners such as the British Classical grammarian,

William Lily (born c. 1468), author of what was the most widely used Latin grammar textbook in England. Although Lily was primarily concerned with explaining Latin grammar, he often went beyond the boundaries of this language, always guided by reason. His attitude was clearly different from, for instance, that of Lindley Murray (born 1745, in Pennsylvania), who wrote a prescriptive grammar of the English language ("how rules should work") inspired in the use of literary authorities. From this other perspective, there is a clear-cut difference between correct and incorrect forms. The former follow a set of rules, and the latter do not. We will come back to this topic later on in the chapter (section 1.2).

I said before that both the Lego blocks and the instructions for assembling them may be essentially the same for every language. Nevertheless, readers may object, observing that languages are definitely very different from each other, at least apparently. Starting from the most obvious facts, two languages such as Basque and English do not share the same words; the lexicon is clearly different in the two languages. Here is an example. An everyday thing such as *bread* is *ogia* in Basque and *job* is *lana*. As we see, there is absolutely no relationship between the languages. *Ogia* has little or no relationship with *bread*, which, on the other hand, is related to German *Brot* and Swedish *bröd*. Of course, it does not mean that English and Basque do not share an important lexical heritage: both have taken many words from Latin and its daughter languages: *literature* is *literatura* in Basque, and *university* is *unibertsitatea*.

Cultural and geographical proximity, therefore, is relevant and explains certain commonalities. Nevertheless, the lexicon of the two languages is still very different. The Lego blocks are different. Clear variances emerge once again when those blocks are connected with one another thanks to grammar, our assembly manual. For example, someone can say: "I have a job." Without getting into details, in this sentence we have a verb (to *have*) and a noun (*job*), which is the object of that verb, and we place them in the following order: V(erb)-O(bject). On the other hand, in standard Basque we say *lana daukat*. In this Basque sentence we have a verb (*eduki* "to have") and a noun (*lana*, which as you will recall means "job" or "work"), but in this case the order changes to O(bject)-V(erb). We will discuss this in further detail in chapter 3. For the time being, one may think, from an Anglocentric perspective, that in Basque one puts the cart before the horse.

And yet, sometimes languages with different words and opposite combinations also agree on matters that are not trivial at all, at least for linguists like myself. Without going too deep into these matters, when we say *Who is this?* or, in Basque, *Nor da hau?*, the first word of the sentence in both languages is the *wh*-word *who*. *Wh*-words are interrogative words, which in English usually start with *wh-* (e.g., *what, which, whose, where*). In Basque, most of these words start with *n-* (e.g., *nor* "who," *non* "where", *noren* "whose") or *z-* (e.g., *zer* "what," *zein* "which," *zenbat* "how much"). Some linguists call these words "*n/z-words*" in Basque. In languages such as English and Basque that exhibit *wh-movement*, sentences containing *wh*-words show a special word order: the *wh*-word appears at the beginning of the sentence, as in the following examples: "Who is there?" "What is the weather like today?" "When is a good time for you?" No English speaker worth his or her salt judges something like **Is who this?* as grammatical—grammarians use asterisks to mark ungrammatical, or, if you wish, badly assembled sentences—and nobody would voluntarily produce a sentence like this. Any English speaker knows that the way to form this sentence is *Who is this?*, fronting the *wh*-word. Thus, two languages such as English and Basque are different regarding word order, one being VO and the other being OV, but both put the *wh*-word at the beginning of the sentence. We will also consider this topic later in the book.

In short, words are different across languages, and the way they are combined also differs sometimes from language to language, but there are times when it does not. In Chomsky's Universal Grammar approach to the study of human language, *principles* refer to certain invariable aspects that all languages share: every sentence must have a subject, for example. In contrast, *parameters* refer to other aspects that may vary from language to language, such as the presence or absence of the *wh*-word at the beginning of the sentence, or whether a verb precedes or follows its object. These parameters do not seem to be arbitrary, and they let us distinguish some languages from others. Understanding them is, for some of us, desirable.

GRAMMAR IS NOT ALWAYS ABOUT CORRECTNESS

The assembly manual that we have been discussing has little or nothing to do with correctness or prescriptive grammar, which, no doubt, is more familiar to educated readers, because of its use in grade school. In the absence of an Academy of the English Language, Merriam-Webster's reference books and dictionaries, along with *The Chicago Manual of Style*, are two of the most influential reference guidelines regarding the rules of English. Today, Merriam-Webster, an institution with a track record of more than a century and a half, is the leading publisher of language reference works for American English. *The Chicago Manual of Style*, on the other hand, is regarded as one of the most prestigious style and usage guidelines and is widely trusted by writers, editors, and the academic community. The ultimate goal of the Merriam-Webster reference works and *The Chicago Manual of Style* is to prescribe and regulate the use of the English language. Instead, here we are going to opt for a more descriptive, and not so prescriptive, approach to language.

Prescriptive grammar is concerned with the proper use of language and seeks to establish a regulated and standard variety, an educated variety, especially in written form. To that aim, this type of grammar bases its rules and prescriptions, for the most part, although not always, on recognized literary authorities. Most of the time, this standard variety differs from the speakers' everyday use of the language. To offer an example, a notable characteristic in African American Vernacular English (AAVE) and some other varieties of the English language, is the so-called *double negation* phenomenon, which consists of allowing negation to be marked in more than one position in the sentence. We will discuss this topic in more detail later on (in chapter 7), but we provide an example in advance. To the question: *Did you get any sleep last night?*, AAVE speakers might answer something like *I ain't get no sleep*, instead of *I didn't get any sleep*. For now, let's say that *I ain't get no sleep* does not belong to the standard variety and, therefore, deviates from standard usage because it contains two negatives in the same phrase. Prescriptive grammarians will insist that double negation is incorrect and should be avoided in formal writing. There are even more stigmatized uses that speakers themselves avoid when acknowledging censors and approving or condemning specific uses of others, often based on the use of their own variety.

Prescriptive grammar, although it is how everyday speakers understand grammar, is obviously neither the only way to do grammar nor the most fun one. Rodney Huddleston and Geoffrey K. Pullum coordinated an excellent reference book on English language grammar: *The Cambridge Grammar of the English Language*, which covers the basic principles of English usage. Each grammar has its own function and rationale, none of which are exclusive. As with everything, it is important to know who does what and when. The Basque language also has an Academy called *Euskaltzaindia*, the Royal Academy of the Basque Language. This academy was in charge of the creation of Standard Basque (or *Euskara Batua*) and its transmission from the early 1960s, as we will see in chapter 6. *Euskaltzaindia* has also produced a standard dictionary of the Basque language, *Euskaltzaindiaren Hiztegia*, under the general editorship of Basque lexicographist Ibon Sarasola. There is also a normative grammar called *Euskal Gramatika: Lehen Urratsak* (Basque Grammar: First Steps), written by the Grammar Commission of *Euskaltzaindia*, now chaired by professor Pello Salaburu of the University of the Basque Country. The goal of the academy is to establish the rules of the Basque language, overcoming dialectal differences, as well as the preservation and transmission of the language.

There is also a superb descriptive Basque grammar in English called *A Grammar of Basque*, written by a team of experts from institutions in the Basque Country, the UK, and the US, and edited by professors José Ignacio Hualde and Jon Ortiz de Urbina. This is a mandatory reference book for anyone interested in the structure of Basque. Furthermore, there are, of course, many additional grammars, such as the volume *Standard Basque* by the late Dutch linguist Rudolf de Rijk, published by MIT Press, and *Sareko Euskal Gramatika* (Basque Grammar Online), among others. As for variation in both morphology and syntax, the database *Basque in Variation (BiV)* is also available online. Let us simply note at this point that some grammar books prescribe the appropriate usage of the language, others describe the way people speak and write, and finally some others attempt to explain the intimate nature of language.

HOW WE UNDERSTAND AND REFLECT ON LANGUAGES

As I said at the beginning of the chapter, our eyes determine the definition we give to an object and not the nature of the object itself. This is also true regarding language. In fact, I am a syntactician (a linguist who studies the Lego assembly or syntax of languages), but not every linguist is concerned with syntax: some linguists are phonologists, who are concerned with sounds; others are lexicographers and analyze words and define them in dictionaries. There are also sociolinguists, psycholinguists, applied linguists, and historical linguists. Linguists like me connect with the Chomskyan rationalist tradition, while some others call themselves empiricists and are concerned only with phenomena that can be observed through the senses. Some of us, without a doubt, prefer deduction as a scientific method, and others declare themselves inductivists. Some of us prefer to ignore the fact that languages evolve, while for others, it is precisely the inexorable passage of time and its drastic consequences that drive them to investigate language. I guess it is like with any other matter in life: some of us are from the city, and some are from the countryside; some of us like coffee, and others prefer tea. Some think that the Napa Valley in California produces better wine than the Columbia Valley in Washington, and others disagree, perhaps vehemently.

All of this might seem funny or trivial, but it is a source of major scientific—and enological—controversy even today. Just to give an example, ignoring the time dimension led twentieth-century researchers to develop an approach to language known as Synchronic Linguistics (from Greek *syn* which means "with," and *chronos*, "time"), which posits that the study of language as a system is independent from the investigation of its historical or diachronic evolution (from Greek *dia*, which means "through," and again, *chronos*, which means "time"). This approach to linguistic research has characterized the last century, as opposed to the historical-comparative or diachronic approach of the nineteenth century. Both approaches to the study of language, synchronic and diachronic (or historical), coexist now. Some other traditions, such as variationist sociolinguistics, bring these approaches together.

Likewise, the rationalist version of grammar, which aims to discover the ultimate nature of human language and its properties through the study of Universal Grammar, is the eternal antagonist of other more down to-earth approaches to the study of language that posit that we can understand the essence of language through our senses and by induction.

But linguists of both persuasions, rationalist and empiricist, are obliged to understand one another. Going back to our comparison above, both the Napa Valley and the Columbia Valley produce excellent merlot. Maybe everything else is arbitrary, banal, and fleeting.

Without mentioning Legos or assemblies, Mark C. Baker, an MIT PhD graduate and a professor of linguistics at Rutgers University, uses a delightful and delicious metaphor to discuss the concept of language in Chomskyan grammar—what is commonly known as Generative Grammar, as well as by other names. Baker writes about Linda, his wife, who apparently is a great cook and likes to bake bread in the oven when they have guests. Yes, once again, our daily bread. Baker says that, after having a dinner with friends, guests always ask Linda for some bread to take home, and she wraps the leftovers. However, sometimes, when just crumbs remain in the bread basket, Linda writes the recipe on a piece of paper. So some bring home a piece of bread and others only the recipe.

When I explain the Bakerian metaphor—of Baker and baking—to my students of Linguistic Typology, a course I teach at the University of the Basque Country that deals with variation in world languages, and I ask them whether the bread recipe is bread or not, a heated discussion often ensues. Some think the recipe is obviously bread and even think it is the very essence of bread. Others, more hesitant and worldly, believe that only bread is bread, and the recipe for baking bread is not bread, period. Still others, more conciliatory and serene, see bread not only in the crumbs but also in the written recipe, and claim that from both the loaf of bread and the recipe we can get a clear notion of what bread truly is.

Let's just say that some linguists like me are the latter, conciliatory ones. Although we know—and this disappoints some of our students—that aside from the nonaggression treaty between the parties, there is to some extent a choice to make between analyzing the loaf and working on the recipe. We must choose one or another methodology to analyze language; in my case, I analyze the recipe. The technical terms that we use to refer to recipe and loaf or slice are, respectively, internal and external language. We speak of internal language as an ability localized in the speakers' mind that allows them to generate grammatical sentences in their language and to distinguish them from ungrammatical ones. The external language, on the other hand, is materialized and perpetuated in texts or emerges in speech and then vanishes if it is not recorded on time. A Chomskyan grammarian prefers the internal language and uses reasoning to understand it. Other linguists do not want to waste their time with abstractions. They prefer to observe the external language and advocate for an extensive search of evidence that lets them construct the facts.

We are both equally (in)dispensable.

BASQUE AND ENGLISH, SUCH DISTINCT LANGUAGES, SO DISTANT, OR SO SIMILAR AND CLOSE

To explain how specialists understand language and languages, we should return to our comparison between English and Basque.

If we consider only the external form of these two languages, the differences between them appear to be huge and the distance between them immense and unbridgeable. There are so many differences that it might just be impossible to list them. Despite this, in terms of internal form, the similarities between both languages are amazing and would stun the most skeptical reader. Leaving aside the fact that they coexist in the minds of bilingual Basque-Americans in Idaho, Nevada, California, and elsewhere, English and Basque are extraordinarily alike when examined at a deeper level because both are different exponents of the same human capability, which makes them necessarily similar. There are closer similarities between any two languages than one would perhaps expect because they all derive from the same universal faculty. Paradoxically then, when reflecting upon English we also reflect upon human language in general. And the same thing happens, of course, when reflecting upon Basque. When we dissect Basque as passionate entomologists, unintentionally, we also do it with English, and vice versa.

Variation among languages is, therefore, strongly constrained by the boundaries of Universal Grammar. Because of these constraints, all languages are essentially alike. At the same time, luckily for variation lovers like me, Universal Grammar also allows languages to vary, even in some of their most intimate and unexplored aspects. Universal Grammar includes parameters that allow for variation. In the setting of some of these parameters, English and Basque differ and are the staunchest enemies, but in others, they run into each other as old friends.

ISOLATED LANGUAGES, RELATED LANGUAGES

Basque and English are also different because they have different historical origins. English is a member of the Germanic family, to which German, Dutch, Afrikaans, Swedish, Norwegian, Danish,

Icelandic, and Yiddish also belong. Families group together with other families, to form larger groups or *phyla*. The Germanic family is included in a very large phylum, Indo-European, which also includes the Italic family, where the Romance languages, Spanish, French, Portuguese, and Italian, among others, belong. Other members of this large phylum also include, for instance, the Balto-Slavic family, which contains languages such as Russian and Polish, and the Indo-Iranian family, including Farsi and Hindi, among many other languages.

Linguists concerned with classifying languages based on their historical kinship represent genetic relationships among languages in the form of language trees, where languages arise as branches from a common stem, and branches may split as new languages develop. Historical linguists hypothesize that about 5,000 or 6,000 years ago there was a language, known as Proto-Indo-European, spoken perhaps in the steppes of Southern Russia and Ukraine, which is the root from which Proto-Germanic sprang as one of the main branches of the tree. The prefix *Proto-* means that this language is not attested in any documents or inscriptions; rather it is an ancestral language reconstructed by linguists. Proto-Germanic, the common mother of all the Germanic languages—yes, we talk about mothers, daughters, etc.—may have been spoken about 500 BCE in northern Germany and southern Scandinavia. Thus, English is one of the daughters of a large, noisy, far-flung, and highly regarded family and has many sisters, cousins, and second cousins.

Basque, on the other hand, has no historical kinship with other languages, or at least none that we know. It could be said that it is an orphan language—a somewhat Dickensian way to look at things—or maybe the only living daughter of unknown parents. Linguists refer to these languages without known relatives as *language isolates*. Basque is a language isolate. Basque is also like a tiny islet that has resisted the pounding of the Indo-European ocean surrounding it for centuries. The result is that we end up with the basic ingredients for an epic poem, probably worth writing.

But if this is brutally true, it is also true that Basque is not the only orphan language on the planet. We are not trying to seek consolation for the uniqueness of others, but curious readers need only check the *Ethnologue* website on world languages (http://www.ethnologue.com/) to verify that several other languages are as isolated as Basque, including, for instance, Burushaski in Pakistan, Purépecha in Michoacan, Mexico, and Warao in Venezuela. These language isolates exist here and there around the world, and we know of others such as Etruscan and Iberian that existed once upon a time and then died off. But of course, being a language isolate is not correlated with being a minority language or even a threatened language. Korean, for instance, is also a language isolate, and it is quantitatively vigorous with more than seventy million speakers. Without reaching the massive number of English speakers (more than 500 million), the number of people who speak Korean is much higher than the modest number of Basque speakers. Basque has about 750,000 native speakers and 430,000 passive speakers. In the most inclusive scenario, Basque has more than one million speakers, which is a fairly large number of speakers among minority languages. To sum up so far: Basque is an isolate, yes, but not the only one; and it is exceptional, yes, or maybe not so much.

WHERE ARE WE?

We have discussed the essential nature of languages, Legos and assemblies, and we have also spoken about other, more earthly matters such as kinship. Some other external matters of language use also preoccupy speakers, especially with minority languages such as Basque. My primary task, and the main goal of this book, is not directly related to issues of language use, but rather to delve into the nature of human language. Nevertheless, linguistic researchers are also human, and, as such, we know the languages we study not only because we observe and analyze them thoroughly and methodically, but also because we love and live with, in, and for them. And as readers might well know, somebody who loves tends to suffer, and plenty. Someone like me cannot possibly be oblivious to the fact that in her neighborhood she can buy the newspaper in Basque at the newsstand and can buy batteries in Basque at the hardware store, but she cannot buy meat in Basque from her beloved butcher, or milk at the supermarket, because nobody there speaks Basque. It is also true, however, that a shop assistant at my patisserie daringly attempts a rudimentary sort of Basque, which cheers my morning every time I go buy a box of cupcakes (and not only because of the cupcakes).

Without taking things to an extreme or being overly dramatic, apparently trivial matters such as deciding in which language to write a scientific article often become important decisions. When I write a scientific paper in Basque, I am aware that I will be able to reach only a tiny readership. To start with, there is only a relatively small number of Basque speakers, and an even smaller number of educated speakers who are used to reading in Basque. And then, of course, very few among them would be interested in reading a specialized article on Basque grammar. If I wrote in English, on the other hand, I know that the number of potential readers would be much greater.

A small language such as Basque has to overcome many hurdles. I am not going to list or analyze them here, not because of cowardice or apathy, but because other people know more about these matters and are trying to find solutions. People like me, explorers on a quest for the most intimate nature of languages, form a small community. The intellectual world that we inhabit is permeated by balance and harmony. This is a world where just a few crazy people, like myself, find happiness.

WHERE ARE WE GOING?

In conclusion, the matter is not so much where we come from, nor where we are, as it is where we are going; each of us should be free to choose. Lego blocks or the instructions for putting them together? Piece of bread or recipe? Induction or deduction? Rationalism or empiricism? William Lily or Lindley Murray?

Synchrony or diachrony? Napa Valley or Columbia Valley? Well, I would like you to continue walking with me along this path, hopefully until the end, and decide for yourself where you want to go.

APPENDIX

The Chicago Manual of Style was first published in 1906 under the title *Manual of Style: Being a compilation of the typographical rules in force at the University of Chicago Press, to which are appended specimens of type in use.* It was one of the first editorial style guides published in the United States. The most recent editions, the sixteenth and seventeenth, published in 2010 and 2017, respectively, have been published in hardcover and online.

Merriam-Webster, founded in 1831 by George and Charles Merriam, is America's most trusted authority on language, having published specialized dictionaries as well as reference books such as *Merriam-Webster's Guide to Punctuation and Style* (published in 1995), *Merriam-Webster's Vocabulary Builder* (1996), *Merriam-Webster's Collegiate Reference Set* (1998), and *Merriam-Webster's Everyday Language Reference Set, New Edition* (2016).

The Cambridge Grammar of the English Language was authored by Rodney Huddleston and Geoffrey K. Pullum and published by Cambridge University Press in 2002.

Euskaltzaindia, the Royal Academy of the Basque Language, has a normative dictionary (*Euskaltzandiaren hiztegia,* The Dictionary of *Euskaltzaindia*), which was coordinated by Ibon Sarasola from the dictionary's inception until recently. Sarasola is developing an online descriptive dictionary named *Egungo Euskararen Hiztegia* (Contemporary Basque Dictionary) [http://www.ehu.eus/eeh/] funded by the Basque Institute of the University of the Basque Country. The basis of the dictionary is the corpus *Ereduzko Prosa Gaur* (Contemporary Prose Reference), which gathers written texts published from 2000 to 2007 and contains more than twenty-five million words. The corpus is also available on the Basque Institute's webpage: [https://www.ehu.eus/eu/web/eins/ereduzko-prosa-gaur-epg-].

The Grammar Commission of *Euskaltzaindia*, now chaired by Pello Salaburu, has been in charge of the development of normative grammar for Basque, *Euskal Gramatika: Lehen Urratsak* (Basque Grammar: First Steps), the most comprehensive set of Basque grammar rules, with a total of seven volumes.

Sareko Euskal Gramatika (Basque Grammar Online) is, as its name indicates, a (descriptive) guide for Basque grammar available online [http://www.ehu.eus/seg/]. Pello Salaburu, Patxi Goenaga and Ibon Sarasola coordinate it.

Readers, the majority of whom do not read Basque, can check *A Grammar of Basque*, a splendid descriptive grammar written by a team of experts from institutions across the Basque Country, the United Kingdom and the United States and edited by José Ignacio Hualde and Jon Ortiz de Urbina, published by John Benjamins in Amsterdam/Philadelphia in 2003.

Rudolf P. G. de Rijk's *Standard Basque: A Progressive Grammar* was published by the MIT Press in 2008. It is, at least in principle, a descriptive grammar with pedagogical purposes, which is particularly interesting for those with previous experience in linguistics and grammar-related issues.

To explore Basque morphosyntactic variation, readers can also visit the online linguistic database *Basque in Variation (BiV)* coauthored by Itziar Orbegozo, Iñigo Urrestarazu, Ane Berro, Josu Landa, and Beatriz Fernández [http://basdisyn. net/Bas&Be/biv/?]. *BiV* was published by the University of the Basque Country (UPV/EHU) in 2018 (second edition), and it is available in both Basque and English. Readers might also consult Koldo Zuazo's *Euskalkiak* (The dialects of Basque) now also available in English [http://euskalkiak.eus/en/].

Mark C. Baker's book, which uses the metaphor about the recipe and the piece of bread, is *The Atoms of Language: The Mind's Hidden Rules of Grammar*, a marvelous and widely read book about the study of linguistic variation written from a Generativist approach. It was published by the Basic Books of New York in 2001. It is an accessible and easy-read.

2

Word Forms:

Languages that Agglutinate or Fuse the Lego Blocks

The Lego blocks: the words. And they condense all of it into a single word. A lot of pieces, definitely, but not so many. Languages that agglutinate the pieces . . . and others that fuse them.

THE LEGO BLOCKS: THE WORDS

As mentioned in the previous chapter, the Basque and English lexicons might at first sight seem nothing alike. Readers will recall that the English *bread* has little or nothing to do with its Basque counterpart *ogia*. English speakers, as well as speakers of other languages, often say that when they start learning Basque, they feel like they are climbing a rock wall without any holds to cling to. However, it is once again the appearance that distinguishes English words from Basque words. On the inside—at least from a Lego maniac's perspective—words in these two languages are indeed more similar than they might seem. Maybe that is why even with a strong will, learning Basque late in our lives might seem arduous, but not impossible. Luckily, many examples demonstrate it is possible. At the end of the day, Basque is one of many natural languages.

We must start somewhere, so forgive me for stating the obvious: both *bread* and *ogia* are words. Readers might be aware that there are still people who believe that some languages do not have the same basic ingredients as other more prestigious languages in the world. Juan Carlos Moreno Cabrera, professor of linguistics at the Autonomous University of Madrid since 1993, addresses this argument in his book *The Dignity and Equality of Languages: Criticism of Linguistic Discrimination.* Regarding Basque, curious readers might try *El Libro Negro del Euskera (The Black Book of Basque)* by Joan Mari Torrealdai, writer, journalist, and member of the Royal Academy of the Basque Language, to visit the museum of horrors that Basque had to overcome throughout its history.

But let's come back to similarities. Both words, *bread* and *ogia*, share the same category: they are both nouns; they are not adjectives, verbs, or any other category. Grade-school knowledge should be enough to discern these categories. Differentiating them is not a trivial matter since it helps us express ourselves in a more accurate and efficient manner.

And now onto the Lego: a noun is a block itself, be it in English, Basque, Quechua, or Farsi. Though the external form differs from language to language, if we were to assemble the Lego set, it would require the same blocks, which are actually placed in the same spots, as we will see later.

In sum, in both English and Basque we have words, and those words form part of the dictionary. That dictionary can be defined through different perspectives. It could refer to the mental dictionary that speakers of any language have in their minds, which allows them to access the necessary words to combine them and finally form sentences. Alternatively, a dictionary can be a book placed in the hands of speakers by lexicographers, like the one Noah Webster wrote for English or Sarasola for Basque. The latter dictionary type is not a mental one that speakers would carry in their minds, which despite its large dimensions is rather light. Instead, it is a physical dictionary that, except in the briefest cases, is much too cumbersome and takes up considerable space in our library. Because time does not stand still, these dictionaries can grow, but paradoxically enough, they can now be accessed through our phones and tablets. In any case, physical dictionaries still exist.

AND THEY CONDENSE ALL OF IT INTO A SINGLE WORD

We need to make a clarification before continuing. Actually *ogia*, even though it is one word, means something other than *bread*. *Bread* differs in that there is no smaller block. *Ogia* is made up of two blocks: *ogi*, which means "bread," and *a*, the definite or indefinite article "the" or "a" in English. That is, *ogia* is not simply "bread" but "the bread" or "a (loaf of) bread." It was not my intention to misguide readers with the explanations given in the previous chapter, but to omit details that might have irritated readers trying to understand the basics. This type of omission will continue, but always within reason.

This finding naturally leads us into another essential stage in our journey, and we illustrate it below so that readers can see it more clearly:

(1)   a. *ogia*
       b. the bread

Indeed, if we count words in both languages, in Basque we have one single world with two blocks: noun and determiner. In English, on the contrary, we have two independent words (noun on the one hand and determiner on the other), neither of which includes a smaller block within. Let us just say that the blocks are basically the same but they are assembled differently.

Let's look at a new example: To the question, "Who did you go on vacation with?", in English we could respond "with my child," while in Basque we would say "*umearekin.*"

(2)   a. *umearekin*
       b. with my child

And once again, we can count the words: one, two, and three in English, but only one in Basque. I do want to clarify that, as we will see later, and apart from a few exceptions, there is no grammatical gender distinction in Basque. In this respect, and although there are differences between both languages, English and Basque are fairly similar. In any case, it is not the presence or absence of grammatical gender that concerns us, but counting words in these two languages.

We continue. Let's assume that we are remodeling our house and we need a hammer. A good Samaritan seeing us struggle might say in Basque:

(3)   a. *Badakarkizut.*
       b. I will bring you one.

And once again, let's count the words: there are five in English while there is only one in Basque. Wow! We can say with one word in Basque what takes five in English. This apparently solitary word has a very vivid inner life that many languages would like for themselves. In Basque everything is clustered within the same word, just like honeybees, which continually work as a team for the betterment of the hive. In English, however, each word is written separately.

A LOT OF PIECES, DEFINITELY, BUT NOT SO MANY

Counting words can be traced back to the nineteenth century when linguists such as Wilhelm von Humboldt began to reflect upon the internal form of words. Without getting into the weeds, some languages, such as Basque, tend to construct complex words that include small blocks that linguists call *morphemes*. Meanwhile other languages, such as English, tend to separate the blocks into independent words. The former are called *synthetic* languages, and the latter are called *analytic* languages. If it is (relatively) true that, comparatively speaking, in Basque certain Lego blocks are synthetic and therefore contain a number of small pieces on the inside, it is also true that Basque sentences contain a lot of pieces, definitely, but not so many. In fact, certain languages are even more synthetic than the synthetic languages themselves; that is, they are the pinnacle of the synthesis and what linguists denominate *polysynthetic* languages. Mark C. Baker, the linguist whose culinary metaphor (the piece of bread and recipe) we discussed in chapter 1, thoroughly studied the nature of polysynthetic languages. In his words, "a polysynthetic language is one that is synthetic to an extreme degree." As a consequence, words in polysynthetic languages are "extremely long and complex, expressing the equivalent of whole sentences in English." Here is one of his illustrations from Mohawk, an endangered Iroquoian language spoken by about 3,500 Mohawk people in southern Ontario and Quebec in Canada, and to a lesser extent in western and northern New York in the United States: Washakotya'tawitsherahetkvhta'se'

The English translation would be "He made the thing that one puts on one's body (i.e., the dress) ugly for her (He uglified her the dress)." Baker explains that it is a somehow forced or unnatural example, something similar to an end-of-vacation suitcase where nothing else fits, but nevertheless not ungrammatical. All in all, if examples from Basque and English are compared, those from Basque are more synthetic. But if we compare examples from Basque and Mohawk, then the Mohawks leave Basque in the dust.

LANGUAGES THAT AGGLUTINATE THE PIECES . . .

In truth, I am presenting the facts out of order. Before talking about synthetic and analytic languages, we usually discuss matters related to word typology and the assembly of blocks, which we also owe to Humboldt, and not so much about the number of blocks that coexist within a word. Here is a previously mentioned example (*umearekin* "child-the-with") to reflect upon. This time, however, the internal form of the word will be analyzed, and the smallest blocks will be identified and separated with a hyphen. For the first time, a word-by-word translation will be added, just like linguists do:

(4)   *ume-a-rekin*
       kid-the-with

Good. This Basque word contains not only three fundamental blocks, but these blocks are also easily identifiable and clearly segmentable. The first small block is the noun *ume* "kid"; the second is the determiner *a* "the," and the third and last piece is *rekin* which corresponds to "with" (we will come back to this in chapter 6, with a more sophisticated analysis). Hence, there is nothing more to do than to choose the appropriate Lego blocks and assemble them together. Below, readers will be asked to create a Basque Lego structure. If readers are given the block *gizon* "man" and is asked to build the Lego structure: "to the man," then the first block to be assembled to the noun is the determiner, resulting in:

(5)   *gizon-a*
      man-the
      "the man"

And then the next block (i.e., *ri*, meaning "to") will be added, resulting in:

(6)   *gizon-a-ri*
      man-the-to
      "to the man"

Readers can practice with *emakume* "woman" as well. To say "to the woman" in Basque, the steps below need to be followed:

(7)   a. *emakume-a*
         woman-the
         "the woman"
      b. *emakume-a-ri*
         woman-the-to
         "to the woman"

That is, the homologue block meaning "to" as well as the remaining blocks are invariable, which allows us to identify and combine these blocks easily.

To continue with the Lego game, if readers are told that "for" in Basque is *rentzat* and is placed in the same place as "to" (*ri*, in Basque), then how would our Basque beginner learners say "for the woman"? As illustrated below:

(8)   *emakume-a-rentzat*
      woman-the-for
      "for the woman"

Since the nineteenth century, these languages that combine smaller blocks to form larger ones have been called *agglutinative* languages, as their morphemes and their boundaries are clearly distinguished. They contrast with the so-called *fusional* languages, where morpheme boundaries are more difficult to identify because they are fused together.

. . . AND OTHERS FUSE THEM

If two of the best-known agglutinative languages are Basque and Turkish, the best-known fusional language is, without a doubt, Latin. It is possible that readers who have studied Latin might remember the first Latin declension: our beloved *rosă, rosae.* Unfortunately, although the departments of classics persevere in the schools of literature, culture, and linguistics at many universities, fewer and fewer young people study Latin. People who attend college in the United States are familiar with Greek letters because of their association with fraternity and sorority names on college campuses (Greek life), but apart from naming the letters and the occasional house motto, these students have little knowledge of Greek altogether. Below, divided in two columns, we illustrate the singular (sg) and plural (pl) forms of a Latin noun belonging to the first declension:

(9) | | sg | pl |
|------------|---------|-----------|
| Nominative | ros-ă | ros-ae |
| Vocative | ros-ă | ros-ae |
| Acusative | ros-ăm | ros-ās |
| Genitive | ros-ae | ros-ārum |
| Dative | ros-ae | ros-īs |
| Ablative | ros-ā | ros-īs |

Each line corresponds to what is known as a *case*. We will consider some of them in chapter 5. It is not our purpose to analyze Latin cases in detail or to intimidate our patient readers.

Let's just remember that we are analyzing words and comparing them across languages. As we have just seen, in agglutinative languages such as Basque, small invariable blocks combine with one another. In Latin, on the other hand, things are very different.

Let's take the form *rosă* as an example. As the table illustrates, *rosă* is simultaneously: a) nominative singular and b) vocative singular. We do not know what each of these forms mean, but we know that one single word can have more than one meaning. *Rosae*, for instance, can be: a) genitive singular, b) dative singular, and to complicate things even more, c) nominative plural and d) vocative plural. Once again, we do not know much about each individual meaning, but one single word can have four different meanings. What is more, if we asked experienced readers to distinguish the little blocks that correspond to case (accusative) and number (plural) in *rosās*, would they be able to do so? Maybe not? Why are readers able to find—and we are confident in the readers— the blocks in *lagunarekin* ("with the friend") but are unable to distinguish the blocks by case and number (and let's not talk about gender) in Latin? Why can readers—complete strangers to Basque at the beginning of the book, who may have even looked at the topic with certain apathy—distinguish the parts of Basque words, but are unable to do so in Latin, which is closer to their native tongue (i.e., English)?

The reason is simple: in languages such as Latin there is no way to separate the parts of words. In Latin, the little blocks do not assemble with one another, but fuse into one. In this case, although at an abstract level we can talk about case and number (or gender) separately, when we observe the word form it is simply impossible to distinguish one block from another. These languages that fuse their blocks are what linguists call *fusional* languages.

APPENDIX

Juan Carlos Moreno Cabrera's book, *The Dignity and Equality of Languages: Criticism of Linguistic Discrimination* was originally published in Spanish in Madrid by Alianza in 2000. This book was republished in 2016 with three new chapters.

An approximation to morphological typology can be found in a number of introductory books to linguistic typology, such as Bernard Comrie's *Language Universals and Linguistic Typology: Syntax and Morphology*, published in 1981.

The characteristics of polysynthetic languages can be revisited in Mark C. Baker's book, cited and recommended in chapter 1 and its appendix.

Joan Mari Torrealdai's piece *El Libro Negro del Euskera* (*The Black Book of Basque*) was published in 1998 by the Ttarttalo publishing company from Donostia-San Sebastián, the Basque Country.

3

The Mirror Image

The mirror image. Object-Verb or Verb-Object, that is the question. Prepositions and mirror images. Assembled blocks that include other assembled blocks. Arranging other Lego blocks: Verb-Auxiliary or Auxiliary-Verb. The subject on the left. (Only) relatively free.

THE MIRROR IMAGE

Readers will recall Lewis Carroll's popular novel *Alice Through the Looking-Glass, and What Alice Found There*, the sequel to *Alice's Adventures in Wonderland*. The youngest readers might be more familiar with an adaptation of the novel as a stand-alone movie or TV show. In the novel, Alice enters an imagined fantasy world, the "Looking-Glass World" by climbing though a mirror where everything is backward: space and direction are inverted, text is reversed, and time runs backward.

> *Then fill up the glasses as quick as you can,*
> *And sprinkle the table with buttons and bran:*
> *Put cats in the coffee, and mice in the tea—*
> *And welcome Queen Alice with thirty-times-three!*
>
> *Then fill up the glasses with treacle and ink,*
> *Or anything else that is pleasant to drink:*
> *Mix sand with the cider, and wool with the wine—*
> *And welcome Queen Alice with ninety-times-nine!*

We do not know whose dream Alice is dreaming. We also do not know whether "Wonderland" exists or not. What we certainly do know is that, all these things aside, English is the mirror image of Basque. In this chapter you will discover why.

OBJECT-VERB OR VERB-OBJECT, THAT IS THE QUESTION

In grammar, when we put together Lego blocks, we normally stop when we get to certain types of verbs, called *transitive* verbs, and their objects: thus, with a verb such as *to read*, we expect to find an object such as *newspaper* or *book* (whether digital or not). Among the few grammar lessons that we may retain from early schooling is the definition of transitive verbs as "those that take an object." Fortunately, this definition works. So, we have two Lego blocks, that is to say, a V(erb) and an O(bject), and in principle, we also have two logical ways to arrange them:

VO or OV, that is the question.

Of course, English speakers will only be able to vouch for VO order since their native language is a VO language. Those English speakers who have studied Spanish or French at school would also have found the same VO order in either of these two other languages.

Consequently, it might be the case that many readers are not aware that the opposite word order, OV, is also attested in other languages of the world. Basque is of this very nature; it is the type of language that any VO-speaker will run into when imagining its mirror image.

(10)   a. To read a book
       b. *Liburu bat irakurri*

It goes without saying that the same thing happens to Basque speakers. Unlike most English speakers reading this book, Basque speakers will usually know at least one language of each type: one OV language (Basque) and one VO language (Spanish or French). The two logical options that allow for arranging the two Lego blocks previously mentioned are thus attested in the languages that reside simultaneously in their heads and take turns when they speak them.

Linguists from several scientific traditions agree in classifying languages as OV or VO. However, they sometimes disagree on the definition of *object*, also known as *complement*. For some linguists, the object or complement of a verb like *to read* is a noun phrase like *a book* or *the newspaper*. Other linguists understand complements as something more abstract: the syntactic position that these noun phrases occupy in the syntactic tree of the sentence. When grammarians build Lego structures, they do not do it to reproduce Indiana Jones' *Temple of Doom* or the Death Star of *Star Wars* but, instead, to represent the internal scaffolding that is intrinsic to languages.

PREPOSITIONS AND MIRROR IMAGES

Sometimes, things have more than one name. This happens with prepositions, which, like nouns or verbs, are syntactic categories. I have already cited some syntactic categories in chapter 2 and will go back to them later. *For* or *in* are only two of the many prepositions in English.

Prepositions have a peculiarity that makes them similar to transitive verbs, mentioned above: all, without exception, require a complement, so that if a preposition appears without its complement, the disassembled block is defective.

(11)   a. For Julia
        b. *For

In the mirror image imagined by English-speaking readers, prepositions are called postpositions and are somewhat like mirror images of prepositions. I do not want postpositions to be tainted by any unreality, or to engage in a philosophical discussion of what is real and what is not. Regarding grammar, prepositions and postpositions, you can call them x or y; either way, they are the same thing. Basically, the crucial difference is that prepositions precede their complements in English, as we already saw, whereas postpositions follow their complements in Basque (12a). Additionally, a postposition cannot be separated from its complement either (12b), since it is not a possible Lego construction:

(12) a. *Julia rentzat*
      b. **rentzat*

What we said about the English preposition *for* or its Basque mirror image *-rentzat* can be extended to any other P (preposition/postposition), such as *of*: once again, P precedes the complement in English, whereas it follows the complement in Basque.

(13) a. **of** you
      b. zu**gan**
         you in

To conclude, let's take a final seemingly small but relevant last step for grammatical theory, referred to as *syntactic theory* by linguists. Both verbs (V) and pre/postpositions (P) are especially important blocks in this Lego grammar. Let's say that other Lego blocks are in their orbit. V and P are known as *heads of phrases*. The word *head* translates as *burua* in Basque. In examples (13a) and (13b), the heads are the English preposition *of* and its Basque counterpart *-gan*. Thus, some linguists do not talk about VO languages or languages with prepositions but, rather, *head-initial* languages (those whose heads are in initial position with respect to their complement, such as English). And they do not talk about OV languages or languages with postpositions either but, instead, about head-final languages (those whose heads are in final position when attached to their object, such as Basque).

ASSEMBLED BLOCKS THAT INCLUDE OTHER ASSEMBLED BLOCKS

We have seen how some blocks link with others and thus form more complex blocks. One of them is the head, which connects with a complement. The Lego in this case is relatively simple:

it only has two blocks. As stated previously, grammarians represent the Lego as a syntactic tree. In this case, the tree has two branches. In the phrase *of you*, for instance, two blocks are linked: the preposition and the pronoun.

(14)   a. of you

b.

of   you

Something very similar, if not the same, happens in Basque, where there are also two blocks: the postposition is the head, and the pronoun is its complement. The order, however, as we already know, is the opposite.

(15)   a. zugan

b.

zu   gan

Let's now assume that we have not only two but three blocks, like in the following example:

(16)   Think of you

As grammarians, we know that these words need to come in a particular order, that is, they are built or scaffolded on one another. Speaking of Legos, each block needs to be stronger than the following one to support the structure. In principle we may assume that the tree-shaped Lego block of *think of you* has three, not two, branches, like the trees above.

(17)

think   of   you

However, this three-branched-tree does not allow for appropriate representation of the internal structure of the complex block since, among other things, it does not reflect the hierarchical relations among the blocks (and moreover the tree cannot grow). For instance, readers know that when we say *think of you* there is, on the one hand, a verb and, on the other hand, a complement that is not solely *of* or solely *you* but a complex block *of you*. To account for this, we prefer a better-articulated Lego structure, one that is jointed in two branches. This is because one of these highest branches extends out to include a new complex block, which in turn branches out into the preposition *of* and the pronoun *you*.

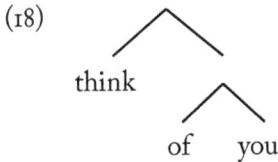

(18)

think

of   you

Thus, the verb *think* connects with a complement, and together they form a complex block that will be called a *phrase*. Since the head of the phrase is a verb, we will then say that this phrase is a *verb phrase*. Because the names of these blocks barely fit in the tree, we will use abbreviations, such as V for Verb or VP for Verb Phrase, and these will be placed in the nodes of the branches.

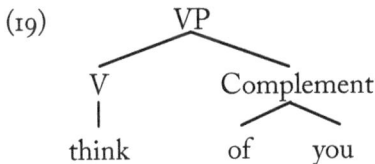

(19)   VP

V   Complement

think   of   you

Let's now look at what we have identified as the complement. Within this complement, there is also a head, even though in this case the head is not a verb, but, rather, a preposition, previously abbreviated as P (an abbreviation that we are using not only for preposition but also for postposition, its mirror image). The preposition *of* also connects to a pronoun *you*, and they together form the type of complex block referred to as a phrase. However, this time it is a *prepositional phrase*, abbreviated PP.

(20)

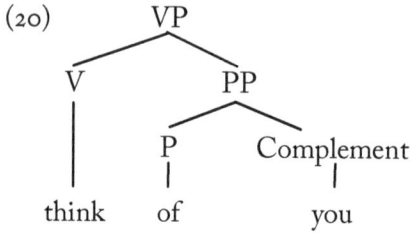

Well, these structures are basically the same in Basque. In a complex block, such as *zugan pentsatu* "think of you," there are three simple blocks (*zu* "you," *gan* "in," and *pentsatu* "to think"). Does the Lego of this complex block have three branches like in (21b)? In Basque, we see, on the one hand, a verb *pentsatu* and, on the other, a complement *zugan* that branches out into two nodes: pronoun and postposition (21c). Adding the corresponding abbreviations to their heads (verb and postposition) and to those of the complex blocks that they build (verb phrase and postpositional phrase), we obtain the Lego block in (21d). This is exactly like the Lego block in English with a single difference: the Lego block in Basque is its mirror image.

(21)   a. Zugan pentsatu

        b.

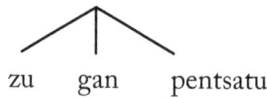

        c.

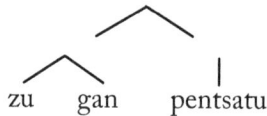

        d.

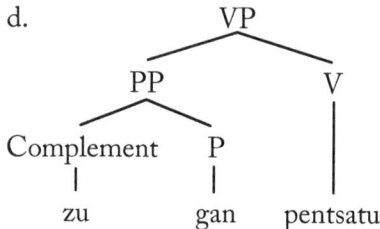

In the mirror image, as we already know, the head is always at the end, as either a verb or a postposition. Therefore, *zugan pentsatu* is something like "you in think" (and not "think in you") with the verb *pentsatu* "to think" following its complement *zugan* "you in," and a postposition *gan* "in" following its complement *zu* "you."

Arranging Other Lego Blocks: Verb-Auxiliary or Auxiliary-Verb

Here I only intend to briefly introduce the nuances of our two languages, English and Basque. For this purpose, I have proposed building some small Lego blocks, growing some small trees.

Readers should not fear that these trees will keep growing and growing, as well as multiplying. They should not rush into giving up this book, nor their commitment to going deep into the somewhat dense woods of grammar. If we continued growing trees, it is likely that we would lose sight of the forest. By the way, these trees are neither oaks nor beeches, but rather baobabs, which branch out under the ground after being planted upside-down and have been punished by the gods for being vain (in this chapter, as can be seen, nothing is straightforward).

Let's assume that we want to make a sentence with *think of you*. In some cases, the sentence would require an auxiliary verb, a topic that we will cover in chapter 4. For instance, in the sentence *I've thought of you*, the verb *to think* is conjugated and accompanied by an auxiliary verb. That auxiliary verb in English is *to have*. The main verb, *thought*, also carries what is referred to as inflection, which will also be covered in chapter 4. Thanks to its inflection, we know, for example, whether a conjugated form is in the present or in the past tense, and, if it is in the present tense, whether it is conjugated in the third-person singular or not. All these matters are classified under the name of inflection. Well, let's add two more branches to our most robust baobab so that it can house the inflection, which will be abbreviated as INFL in the tree.

(22) a. I have thought of you

b. INFL   VP

            V   PP

                P   Complement

have   think   of   you

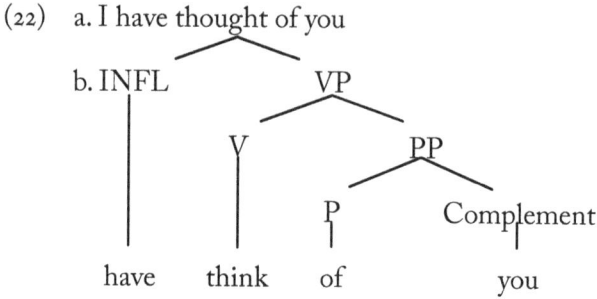

Let's now examine its corresponding form in Basque: *zugan pentsatu dut* "you in thought have." Readers already know some of these blocks. The only one that has not been presented yet is the last one, that is, *dut*. In Basque, *dut* is a form of the auxiliary verb "to have." In Basque, this auxiliary carries the inflection and expresses person, number, tense, and mood. In English there is less overt inflection: the third-person singular carries inflection in the auxiliary verb *has*, but the rest of the paradigm shows no inflection: *I have, you have, we have, they have.* Another important difference between the two languages is the position of the auxiliary with respect to the rest of the blocks: in Basque, the auxiliary is found, of course, in final position.

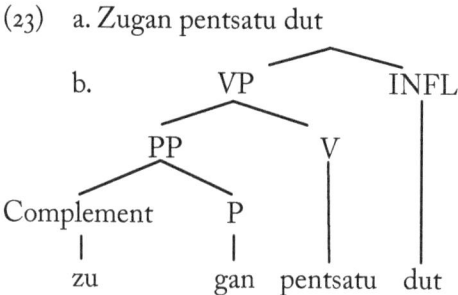

(23) a. Zugan pentsatu dut

b.   VP   INFL

        PP   V

Complement   P

   zu   gan pentsatu dut

And once again, Basque is the mirror image of English. However, sometimes that mirror image is diluted, and Basque is identical to English.

THE SUBJECT ON THE LEFT

With our last two baobabs, which are simply one and its own mirror image, just like before with prepositions and postpositions, we now almost have a complete Lego. We want to remind readers that for syntacticians, there is no life beyond the boundaries of a sentence. Or if there is, syntacticians still care primarily about sentences.

However, before building the Lego of a sentence, the subject needs to be crafted into a branch, and that is what we will do next. It is a fact that when we say *I've thought of you*, there is a subject "I" that we know needs to be explicit in English and needs to have its own place in the tree.

That subject is placed to the left of the inflection and the rest of the blocks. Because we are already familiar with the structure of the verb phrase or VP, we put the VP under a triangle. This triangle lets us omit its previously identified nuances and concentrate on the rest of the blocks. When the subject is added to the Lego, we finally obtain the complete sentence, represented in the root node of the tree as S.

(24) a. I have thought of you

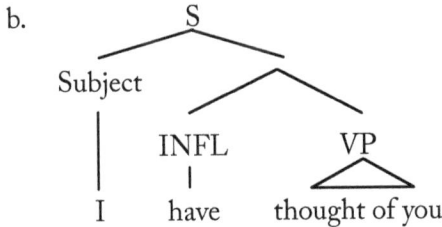

b.
```
                  S
          _____|_____
       Subject        ___/\___
          |          /        \
          |        INFL        VP
          |         |         /\
          I        have   thought of you
```

Well, where is the subject in that mirror image language? Against all odds, it is in the same position as the subject in English in a right-side up world. In many ways, the Basque language is the reverse image of English: regarding the position of its syntactic heads, such as verb and P, with respect to its complements, and in regard to the order of the subject and the rest of the sentence. In one way, however, English and Basque are exactly alike: both languages have the subject on the left.

(25)   a. Zugan pentsatu dut

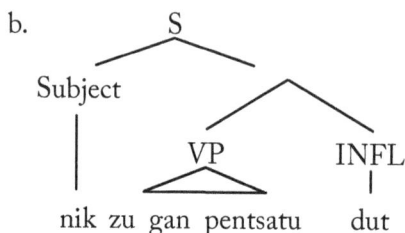

b.

```
                    S
           _____/_____
       Subject              /\
         |                 /   \
         |               VP      INFL
         |              /\        |
      nik zu gan pentsatu        dut
```

Less Legomaniac linguists than I would express things more directly, without beating around the bush: one is a VO language (English) and the other is an OV language (Basque), but both are S(ubject)-V(erb) languages. No matter how you put it, remember that the subject, like the heart, is always on the left.

(ONLY) RELATIVELY FREE

We are getting close to the end of this chapter, which is shorter than the ones following it, as it is arduous traveling from the real to the dream world and, even more so, traveling through baobab forests. The baobabs show us that, regarding word order, the syntactic reconciliation between English and Basque is frankly difficult, if not impossible, but that at least, both languages agree on the position of the subject in the phrase. It is better than nothing.

Another matter regarding word order in which the two languages disagree is in how much word order freedom each of them allows its speakers. Freedom of word order means that, even though there is a word order that we grammarians call "canonical" or "unmarked," the canonical order can be altered and transformed. Readers can simply call it normal order, which is the order in which things are usually arranged. This unmarked order can turn into marked order without resulting in a poorly constructed or defective Lego. Pieces, therefore, move around with a certain supervised freedom, like in the following example in Basque (and without glosses):

(26) a. Nik zugan pentsatu dut
       b. Zugan pentsatu dut nik
       c. Pentsatu dut nik zugan
       d. Zugan nik pentsatu dut
       e. Nik pentsatu dut zugan
       f. Pentsatu dut zugan nik

The canonical order is presented in (a), which has already been analyzed. Nonetheless, the rest of the examples above are just as grammatical. There are some differences in the nuances of meaning among them, such as that it was "me" and not another one who thought of you (e), or that I thought of "you" and not another person (d), etc. Ultimately, what matters is that each one of those attested word orders is grammatical. In comparison, English allows less freedom:

(27) a. I have thought of you
       b. Of you, I have thought
       c. * Have thought I of you
       d. *Of you have thought I
       e. *I of you have thought
       f. *Have thought of you I

The greater freedom that Basque allows is, of course not unlimited. It is not the case that any word order is allowed in Basque either. The following examples are also not possible in Basque:

(28) a. *Pentsatu nik zugan dut
       b. *Zugan pentsatu nik dut

We may conclude that both languages, therefore, are (only) relatively free in terms of their word order, with English having less freedom in this respect than Basque. Some of the effects that are obtained in Basque by moving the words around the sentence can be expressed in English by giving greater emphasis to different words: *I have thought of you, I **have** thought of you, I have **thought** of you, I have thought of **you**.*

APPENDIX

Lewis Carroll's novel *Alice Through the Looking-Glass, and What Alice Found There*, edited by John Tenniel and Fritz Kredel, was published by Macmillan and Co. in London in 1872. Since then, more than six hundred editions have been published in different formats. This novel is the sequel to the globally famous book *Alice's Adventures in Wonderland* (Macmillan, 1866). *Alice's Adventures in Wonderland* was a huge success at a time when most children's books were dreary, tedious instructional books with a religious moral message. Alice sprang as a witty, humorous, and imaginative character that conquered the hearts of children and adults of Victorian times.

Reverend Charles Lutwidge Dodgson (1832–1898), better known by his pen name Lewis Carroll, was a timid mathematician and Anglican deacon at Christ Church, Oxford. He shared a very affectionate relationship with the three eldest daughters of Reverend Henry George Liddell, the dean of his Church. Most of the characters the author depicted in his books were based on people he knew or met during his life. Alice was his favorite daughter of the three that he constantly entertained with his puzzles, games, and stories. She eventually became the heroine of his tales.

4

An Emergency Manual or Overview

on the Sophisticated Nature of

Verbal Inflection in Basque

Verbal inflection in Basque: a sophisticated machinery. Synthetic and analytic verb forms in synthetic and analytic languages. What inflection hides (and what it does not): arguments and adjuncts, leading and supporting roles. The rebellion of the adjuncts. *Ki* and a small recess. Certain outliers with odd names sneak into inflection: the allocutives. Auxiliary verbs and analytic forms. Intransitives vs. transitives. Participles accompanied by auxiliaries.

VERBAL INFLECTION IN BASQUE: A SOPHISTICATED MACHINERY

At this point, readers are already almost experts, which allows us to get into obscure territory, even for me, despite having worked on this subject matter for years. Even today, I dedicate intense hours to studying it, which usually end in terrible and paralyzing migraines. While not wishing to put readers through this suffering, I want them to experience the joy of discovering some of the secrets of this machinery called *verbal inflection* in Basque, which has already been briefly mentioned in the previous chapter.

Readers might once again, and with good reason, ask themselves what verbal inflection is. Well, verbal inflection is everything you add to a verb, such as *to bring*, when it is conjugated.

Some conjugated forms of the verb *to bring* are, for instance, *brings* or *has brought*, with their respective forms *dakar* or *ekarri du* in Basque. Because of inflection, we know that in Basque, there is a subject and who that subject is, such as first-person singular or plural. We also know whether, in addition to this subject, there is a direct or indirect object; we know if the verb is conjugated in the present tense or not; we know if it is indicative or subjunctive; we know whether it is perfective or imperfective; we know who the interlocutor is and their degree of familiarity with respect to the speaker; we know the gender, male or female, of the interlocutor too. All this is thanks to this sophisticated machinery with secrets that still remain hidden and well-secured.

SYNTHETIC AND ANALYTIC VERB FORMS IN SYNTHETIC AND ANALYTIC LANGUAGES

Among the aforementioned conjugated forms, we can distinguish synthetic and analytic verb forms. Readers might remember that in a synthetic language such as Basque, a single word contains a lot of morphemes, whereas English, which is an analytic language, separates those morphemes into more than one word. The point is that, regarding verbal inflection, it seems that synthetic and analytic forms can be found in both languages. Let's look at an example. In Basque, a verb such as *to know* "jakin" has synthetic forms. Thus, the third-person singular in the present tense, referring to "she/he knows," would be:

(29) daki

This form is synthetic because it is expressed in a single word. But it is also true that the equivalent verb in English is also synthetic.

(30) knows

Basque has also analytic verb forms, that is, forms that include a main lexical verb and an auxiliary, as in English (we will analyze these forms in section 4.7).

(31)   a. jakin du
       b. has known

The differences arise when comparing other synthetic forms in Basque to their equivalents in English. For instance:

(32)   a. dakart
       b. I bring

Here we need two words in English to translate a single word in Basque. Moreover, if we are more thorough, we might say that the equivalent of *dakart* is not merely *I bring*, but rather:

(33)   a. dakart
       b. I bring it

And in Basque we could even say:

(34)   a. dakarkizut
       b. I bring it to you

That is, it takes three, or even five, words in English to express what takes only one to say in Basque. Although synthetic forms are much more common in Basque than in English, we do find a few comparable examples in English, in which the verb and the direct object merge into one word. Some of these forms are used in both oral and written contexts, such as (34), while others are part of nonstandard speech and are restricted to oral, informal contexts, such as contractions:

(35)   a. let's
       b. bring 'em

In English, it is also possible to informally merge the verb or modal verb with a preposition:

(36)   a. gonna
       b. gotta
       c. wanna

English also allows one to integrate negation within the main verb (37), the modal verb (38) or the auxiliary verb (39), which is another way of merging various morphemes into a single word. Contractions have an informal, colloquial character, and these forms are commonly used only in oral speech, especially the vernacular form *ain't*. These are examples of synthetic forms in English. A major difference between these languages is that Basque can consistently integrate a higher number of morphemes into its verbs than English.

(37) ain't

(38) won't

(39) a. doesn't
b. didn't
c. haven't

WHAT INFLECTION HIDES (AND WHAT IT DOES NOT): ARGUMENTS AND ADJUNCTS, LEADING AND SUPPORTING ROLES

Verbal inflection in Basque hides a number of morphemes, some of which are related to what are called the *arguments* of a verb. The term *argument*, in this context, has little to do with the definition that readers will most likely have accessed in their mental dictionaries, or even in libraries, unless these libraries contain technical linguistic dictionaries. When I explain what arguments are in graduate linguistics seminars, I usually reference actors from movies. Let's say that arguments are the protagonists of the movie, and without those actors, the filming would simply be canceled. Other actors, nonetheless, are supporting actors whose acting careers are more fragile and ephemeral. The former are known as arguments while the latter are *adjuncts*. If a lead actor disappears, the filming is canceled. If a supporting actor disappears, however, even the makeup artists would not notice. Therefore, a phrase could be compared to an abstract movie in which there are lead and supporting actors who, not long ago, were also known as secondary. Through dedication, professionalism, and good work, the secondary actors have accomplished the more deserving label of "supporting actors."

As a film enthusiast myself, I do not wish to emphasize the differences between lead and supporting actors. However, certain movies have a clear and unique protagonist, which in the context of syntax, would be a phrase with a single argument. For instance, in the newest *Wonder Woman* (Patty Jenkins, 2017), undisputable heroine Diana, an Amazonian warrior who leaves home to fight in the war, is played by the magnificent Gal Gadot. The details of the movie will not be discussed here. Those who have seen it will pleasantly recall the story, and those who have not will hopefully have the opportunity to do so. We will not praise Gadot's splendid interpretation either, even though her performance was highly acclaimed by critics.

For Gadot's story in the context of syntax, there would be a verb known as *intransitive verb*. That is, it has only one argument, which is also the subject of the sentence. Intransitive verbs are, for example, *to be* (*fed up with*), *to go* (home), or *to come* (from the impound), and in these cases, there is only one argument in the inflection:

(40) a. nago
     b. noa
     c. nator

In English, unlike in Basque, the subject needs to also be overtly expressed because verbs in this language cannot stand alone except for a few instances, such as imperatives:

(41) a. I am
     b. I go   b'. Go!
     c. I come   c'. Come!

In the history of the Academy Awards, a notably emotional moment accompanied *On Golden Pond* (1981, Mark Rydell). The movie's plot revolves around Norman Thayer (Henry Fonda) and his wife, Ethel (Katharine Hepburn), who spend their summers at a New England vacation cottage on the shores of paradisiacal

Golden Pond. One summer, their daughter, Chelsea (Jane Fonda), visits them with her fiancé and son on their way to Europe, and she attempts to repair her troubled relationship with her aging father before she regrets it. Henry Fonda won his only Academy Award for Best Actor at the age of seventy-six, becoming the oldest winner in this category. Sadly, he was unable to attend the ceremony because of heart disease. Instead, Jane Fonda, his daughter and costar, accepted the Oscar on his behalf. He died five months after receiving the award. Later, Jane confessed that the father-daughter relationship portrayed in the movie was very similar to their real-life relationship and that the movie helped them repair it before her father lost a long battle with heart disease. The two-time Academy Award winner Jane Fonda was not as highly praised as the other two protagonists, her father and Hepburn, but without her, the relationship between the characters would not have been as genuine or transcendent. She might have also partly been the reason why her father was awarded an Oscar for that passionate and heartwarming performance.

In some movies, with or without awards, there is more than one main character. It is difficult to imagine the scene where one acts without the other, which in this example is the antagonist, as shown below.

Truth be told, analyzing sentences is not as exciting as watching a movie that received three Oscars and three Golden Globes. However, the metaphor may serve as a little tribute to an exceptional movie and to help readers recall more common notions. One such notion is that verbs have two arguments, one of which is the subject and the other the object, both being hidden in the inflection like a well-kept secret. These verbs are, for example, *eduki* "to have," *eraman* "to carry," or *ekarri* "to bring," and the following verbs are conjugated forms of these infinitives.

(42) a. naukazu
      b. naramazu
      c. nakarzu

In these sentences, which could be translated as follows, *na* corresponds to the object and *zu* to the subject:

(43)   a. youhaveme or yougotme
      b. youbringme
      c. youtakeme

And even with the intransitive verbs mentioned before, there might be another individual alongside the protagonist subject. Then, there is not only one but two arguments, and even though the main character is the subject, another actor, who is not a lead or an extra, sneaks into the inflection. Thus, in Basque, we say:

(44)   a. nagokizu
      b. noakizu
      c. natorkizu

Which might roughly correspond to:

(45)   a. Iamtoyou
      b. Igotoyou
      c. Icometoyou

We merge words not to annoy honorable scholars but to teach readers the perspective with which we work, and which allows us to determine the closest similarities, if any, between both languages. In either a single word or multiple words (that is, according to prescriptive grammar), these forms might bother English speakers, or they might consider them defective or ungrammatical. Without going into detail, readers will come up with strategies to improve forms such as *I come to you* by adding *to see.* That is to say, *I come to see you.* A verb such as *noakizu/I come to you* is nothing more than *I, Simon, come to (see) you.* It is that simple.

In addition to *Wonder Woman* or *On Golden Pond*, another splendid movie worth noting is *Loreak* (Jon Garaño and Jose Mari Goenaga, 2014), presented at the sixty-second edition of the San Sebastián International Film Festival. A remarkable fact about this movie is that it was not filmed in Spanish or English like most movies at this festival, but instead, it was filmed in Basque. It was an absolute honor for the Basque community to see a movie entirely filmed in our language and chosen to be included in the Official Section for the second time in the festival's history. The Academy of Arts and Sciences also selected this movie to compete for Best Foreign Language Film in the eighty-eighth Academy Awards. *Loreak* means "flowers" (or "the flowers" or "some flowers," but most importantly, it is flowers, regardless of *how on earth*—as we say in Basque, *nola demontre*—they are determined).

In this third movie, it is not a Diana saving the world from a villain, or a father and a daughter saving their relationship before it is too late. In *Loreak*, three protagonists' fates intertwine because of the flowers: beloved veteran Itziar Aizpuru, winner of a Feroz Award, and two other actresses, Itziar Ituño, who won a Toulouse Cinespaña award, and Nagore Aranburu, who has not been awarded a prize yet. Aranburu's role, however, was essential and her professionalism impeccable. In this movie, there are not two but three women bearing the brunt of a drama that is drawn-out, but also seasoned with suspense. Once again, syntax is more trivial for the average citizen (than for us), but the point is to determine the nature of the selected verb, and, consequently, how many protagonists there are this time.

Verbs, such as *eraman* "to take" or *ekarri* "to bring," were previously described as transitive verbs. However, these verbs can appear not only with two arguments, subject and object, but also with three, by adding an indirect object to the other two arguments. In other words, apart from saying who brings what, they may also express who brings what to whom. Verbs with three arguments (who, what, and to whom) are usually classified as *ditransitive verbs*. Once again, because inflection is wise, there are three protagonists in the phrase. All three of them are sheltered in the core in such a way that in Basque one finds forms such as:

(46) a. dakarkiozu
      b. daramakiozu

which correspond to the following forms in English:

(47) a. youbringitforher
b. youtakeittohim

Properly written as: *you take it to her* or *you bring it to him.* Note that the third-person singular pronouns and possessives in Basque are gender-neutral, which means that *he* and *she*, as well as *his* and *her,* have one single-neuter equivalent in Basque. For the sake of consistency and because the feminine equivalent often comes second to the masculine one, "she" and "her" will be used in the following examples. Bear in mind, however, that these are interchangeable with "he" and "him."

THE REBELLION OF THE ADJUNCTS
As previously discussed, inflection hides protagonists, such as the subject, the direct object, and even the indirect object. However, within inflection, adjuncts have a hard time finding shelter, and thus, these adjuncts are by definition condemned to anonymity and oblivion. Therefore, one can say, for instance:

(48) a. Zurekin doa
b. (She) goes with you

But inflection does not really care who goes with whom nor does it change for this reason, be it with you or with John.

(49) a. Jonekin doa
b. (She) goes with John

As can be observed, nothing seems to change the inflected verb form: it can accompany "she" or "Jon," being *doa* in Basque and *goes* in English. In the previous sentences, *Jonekin* or *with John* are adjuncts and, as another example, *autoan* or *by car* in the following ones:

(50) a. Autoan doa
b. (She) goes by car

Once again, the inflected form *doa/goes* does not change in the presence of adjuncts, which can even be substituted without seemingly affecting the grammaticality of the sentences:

(51)   a. Goizez doa
        b. (She) goes in the morning

Of course, this also happens with transitive sentences. We can add as many adjuncts as we want to these constructions, but they cannot be sheltered in the scope of inflection:

(52)   a. Sagarra dakar zuretzat/Jonentzat
        b. (She) brings an apple for you/for John

Zuretzat/for you or *Jonentzat/for John* are also adjuncts.

Sometimes, though, the most oppressed revolt and, during the riot, achieve a power of which they had never dreamed. In those cases, adjuncts become arguments, and not just any arguments: the rebels rise through the ranks to become objects. As a result, the number of arguments in the phrase increases.

These syntactic riots, which in linguistic typology and grammar are also known as *applicative constructions*, are frequent in Bantu languages (in Africa), Austronesian languages (in the Western Pacific region), and Salishan, Mayan, and Uto-Aztecan languages (in Northern and Central America).

Data from these languages with applicative constructions will not be provided here, because that would overcomplicate the text. However, I do want to present these constructions in a way that readers can understand, even if they do not speak these languages. Let's consider again the last sentence we have just discussed:

(53)   (She) brings an apple for John

This phrase consists of a conjugated transitive verb (*to bring, brings*), an object (*an apple*), and an adjunct (*for John*), which has a *benefactive* role, meaning that it is probably he/John who will eat the apple, for instance, a Granny Smith. Instead, if we had the poisoned apple of the Evil Queen and the *goal* of the action were to kill poor Snow White, then we would be talking about a *malefactive.* The benefactive case is syntactically one of the farmers or ironsmiths confronted with the socially favored high-class subjects and objects in the phrase. But during a riot, it could be the case that the stigmatized adjunct with the preposition *for* abandons the stigma, the preposition merges with the verb form (known as *applicative* morpheme), and the rioter John occupies the canonical object position located immediately after the verb in English.

(54) a. (She) forbrings John an apple
      b. *(She) forbrings an apple John

(54a) is a hypothetical applicative construction in an also hypothetical English-Bantu language. In the sentence, the preposition *for* no longer precedes *John*. Instead, the preposition merges with the verb form, becoming an applicative morpheme, and John is now in the object position. In fact, these exotic applicatives can also be found, if we pay attention, in some words of the English lexicon. For instance, you can either say that *the army takes over the village* or merge the preposition with the verb and say that *the army overtakes the village.*

When *John* becomes the new object of the applicative construction, the apple, the former (direct) object of the phrase, faces two not very flattering scenarios: (i) sometimes, it turns into a *chômeur*, a French word meaning "unemployed," which in grammar is used to refer to an element that has been syntactically demoted from the nucleus. That is, as if somebody had taken away his job, left him unemployed, and he had lost not only a well-deserved salary but all his privileges as the object of the sentence—for example, in the presence of the rebel, the apple can hardly occupy his former object position (54b); (ii) in other cases, in not such adverse circumstances, it is the second in command in the list of objects in the phrase, always contingent on the rebel object. These cases have been documented in certain languages and are also grammatical (54b). Another privilege that the rioter would acquire is the ability to be pronominal inside the inflection. Our hypothetical English-Bantu would result in forms such as (55a):

(55)   a. (S)he forbroughtit an apple
        b. *(S)he forbroughtit John

In (55a), *John* is omitted and the object pronoun *it* appears. Thus, the *unemployed* apple would not have access to and could be neither omitted nor pronominalized.

Furthermore, the rioter John who became the object of the phrase ousting apples, Granny Smith or not, poisoned or not, can continue with the riot and even become the subject of a passive sentence constructed upon a previous applicative phrase (that is to say, one merged with the *for* preposition):

(56)   a. John is forbrought an apple
        b. *An apple is forbrought John

Once again, the apple would be adversely affected in this internal struggle. This apple could not aspire to be the subject of a passive sentence in the presence of a rebel syntactically raised by the applicative.

I have not brought up these hypothetical examples to offend the linguistic conscience of plurilingual English-speaking readers, among whom, luckily, maybe there is a small number who also have linguistic conscience in Bantu, Mayan, or Uto-Aztecan. However, I do wish for readers to know that there are languages in which the prepositions that precede adjuncts, the so-called supporting roles, merge with inflection and jeopardize the pre-established syntactic hegemony. These rebel adjuncts are sometimes benefactive, such as *for John*, but can also be comitative (*with John*), instrumental (*with the ax*), and even locative (*in the water*). After the riot, nonetheless, all of them, without exception, are objects. That is to say that they are now one of the main protagonists of the sentence.

KI AND A SMALL RECESS

If I have tested the readers' nerves when previously discussing applicative constructions, it is not because I have nothing better to do, but because at the core of Basque verbal inflection, there is a chameleonic morpheme that is similar to these constructions. I will arbitrarily call it *ki* since the morpheme has appeared in this form in each and every example in Basque considered throughout this chapter. For now, I will omit the many names given to this glitch of Basque grammar. Here are some of the examples we have already seen:

(57)   a. noa**ki**zu
        (I)gotoyou
      b. nator**ki**zu
        (I)cometoyou

(58)   a. dakar**ki**ozu
        (you)bringittoher
      b. darama**ki**ozu
        (you)takeittoher

These are already well-known examples, but until now, I have deliberately ignored the presence of *ki*, despite it clearly appearing in every example. In fact, this morpheme is another key piece in our puzzle.

Even though the theoretical status of this morpheme has not been adequately discussed except for a few exceptions, it is similar to the applicative or, in other words, the merged prepositions of Bantu and other languages. *Ki* invariably precedes certain added arguments that can only be sheltered by inflection if preceded by this morpheme. Conjugated verb forms that include *ki* without introducing a new argument are just as ungrammatical. This can be seen in the following examples:

(59)   a. noa
        (I)go
      b. noa**ki**zu
        (I)gotoyou
      c. *noazu
      d. *noaki

The example (59a) is a verb form with one single argument; (59b) consists of a subject, a second argument *zu* (second-person singular *to you*) preceded by *ki*, that is, roughly *goes-preposition-you*; (59c) is incorrect because *ki* is absent in the presence of the added argument *zu*; and finally, (59d) is also incorrect, but in this case, it is because *ki* is present while the added argument is absent. Similar examples are provided in (60), this time using the verb *to bring*.

(60) a. dakar
      (she)bringsit
      b. dakar**ki**o
      (she)bringsittoher
      c. *dakar**ki**
      d. *dakarro

Is this an applicative, that is to say, a merged preposition *à la* Bantu? I am not certain, but it probably is. What I do know without a doubt is that no analysis can prevent the presence of this morphological animal that is seemingly inert, but syntactically alive.

CERTAIN OUTLIERS WITH ODD NAMES SNEAK INTO INFLECTION: THE ALLOCUTIVES

Sometimes certain outliers that are not arguments of the sentence, that is, neither subjects nor objects, sneak into Basque inflection. These outsiders are not the heroes of the riot either. They are born relegated to the syntactic periphery and achieve power by ousting some of the main protagonists.

Let's say that these nonargument outliers are related to something that transcends sentences and even syntax. They are elements that put us in a certain communicative situation where, when we talk, we inevitably must address an interlocutor in a specific way. By using these elements, when we say, for instance, that someone is coming, brings something, or brings it to somebody, we add to the inflection both who it is said to and the degree of familiarity with which it is done. By a whim of nature that sometimes bestows gifts upon us mortals in amazing and almost unimaginable ways, Basque inflection distinguishes gender of the listener, even if it is a mostly grammatical gender-free language. Basque does not have morphological gender, unlike Spanish or French, but it contains exotic verb forms that include a particular morpheme for that interlocutor and distinguishes their gender. These (always) attractive outliers are called *allocutives*.

Thus, some forms, which have already been analyzed and are translated once again below, have their corresponding allocutive forms, in the masculine form (*k*) if the interlocutor is masculine (examples 61b, 62b, and 63b) and the feminine form (*n*) if the interlocutor is feminine (examples 61c, 62c, and 63c).

(61)   a. dator "(s/he) comes"
        b. ziatorre**k**
        c. ziatorre**n**

(62)   a. Dakar "(she) brings"
        b. ziakarre**k**
        c. ziakarre**n**

(63)   a. dakarkio "(she) brings it to her"
        b. ziakarkio**k**
        c. ziakarkio**n**

These allocutive forms indicate a certain degree of familiarity with the interlocutor, which does not necessarily happen with all allocutives. For this reason, they are pragmatically ruled and cannot be used with just anybody in any way without running the risk of being impolite or even disrespectful and outraging the interlocutor. Not only is the exquisite morphological architecture of these verb forms fascinating, but the social and pragmatic web that rules their use is as well. Allocutives are attested to in the main dialectal areas of Basque, that is, western, central, and eastern dialects, although they are more frequently used in some varieties than in others. Even standard Basque has its normative use of allocutives.

Maybe we should openly say that, in this respect, Basque and English are definitely different—and, by the way, Basque allocutives are very similar to Japanese honorifics. It might even seem like there is no way to learn, process, or let alone produce these forms. However, the minds of the Basque speakers who possess this treasure in their dialects are neither wilder nor luckier than any English speaker's mind. This means that speakers of any language can learn the allocutive system of Basque. Children, for example, master it with absolute spontaneity and without effort or training. With discipline, dedication, and perseverance, adults can as well.

AUXILIARY VERBS AND ANALYTIC FORMS

So far, most of the Basque forms presented in this chapter are synthetic, and thanks to our poetic-grammatical license, so are the English forms that we have provided in the glosses. In any case, verb forms such as *(I) am*, *(you) have*, or *(she) brings* are also synthetic forms known in grammar as *simple* forms (even though they are not simple at all). Simple forms are different from analytic forms, better known as *compound* forms in the field of grammar and referred to as *periphrastic* forms in Basque grammar. Three names for one thing? Well, yes, life is capricious and so is the lexicon. In Basque analytic forms, transitive verbs take the auxiliary verb **edun* "have," whereas intransitive ones take the auxiliary verb *izan* "be." Analytic (or periphrastic or compound) forms are the following in Basque:

(64) a. egon naiz
      b. joan naiz
      c. etorri naiz

Their equivalents in English:

(65) a. (I) have been
      b. (I) have gone
      c. (I) have come

Both forms in Basque and English share one feature: they all include an *auxiliary verb*, thanks to which one can conjugate verbs (relatively) freely and say things like *has been*, *had been*, etc. There is a curious thing about the auxiliary verb. It may seem that the fundamental part of the sentence is the verb, but for Legomaniacs such as ourselves, the verb is a lexical block. It is an important block, but maybe not as important as the auxiliary block. This block allows for the articulation of all the inflection and, therefore, the sentence, when, who knows why, *everything does not fit* in a synthetic form and it must be broken in two. Thus, "auxiliary," like "adjunct," is an unfair label that we unwillingly tolerate since the poor little words are busy enough prodigiously encapsulating the universe and thus enabling us to articulate our sentences.

In perfective forms, certain languages such as Spanish, Portuguese, and some Catalan varieties select the auxiliary *to have*, whereas other languages such as Gaelic, Scottish, or Tamil select *to be*. However, there are other languages, such as French, Italian, Occitan, German, Dutch, Medieval Portuguese, and Medieval Gaelic that select both auxiliaries, that is, *to have* and *to be*. At least in this respect, Basque is more similar to French, its other neighbor, than to Spanish.

(66)   a. joan naiz
           gone am
        b. eraman dut
           taken have

And we do not say, as in English or Spanish:

(67)   *joan dut
         gone have

This BE-HAVE alternation even existed in English centuries ago, as documented in the well-known Christmas song "Joy to the World," originally written by the British theologian Isaac Watts in 1719: "Joy to the world, the Lord *is come*, let Earth receive her king."

However, English speakers might have forgotten that this alternation once existed and might need to consider French or Italian to understand auxiliary alternation in Basque.

INTRANSITIVES VS. TRANSITIVES

Having seen the examples given in (66), readers have probably guessed that the alternation of auxiliaries I talked about is essentially based on the distinction between intransitive and transitive verbs: intransitives, those with a single protagonist, select the verb *to be*, whereas transitives, those with multiple protagonists, select the verb *to have*. This means, of course, that this happens in Basque but not in English, which selects *to have* without distinction as we saw earlier.

I must clarify that when I say that the auxiliary verbs *to be* and *to have* alternate in Basque, obviously, I do not mean to say that these auxiliaries are exactly the ones we find in Basque but the equivalents in Basque. Specialized literature uses the English auxiliaries BE and HAVE, in capital letters, to refer to auxiliaries in general without mentioning any particular language. We could do the same, and we suspect that readers would even approve of it, but we do not deem it necessary in a book like this. Moreover, as readers, we have a somewhat egocentric perception of our own language, especially when it is one of the most powerful. Speakers of minority languages, including Basque, tend to be a bit humbler about it and are not used to making headlines, or at least not for anything good.

But let's return to the languages whose structures (but not lexicons) are, in principle, independent from these worldlier matters. Some of the intransitive verbs that have already been presented will be repeated below.

(68) a. egon naiz
      been am
      b. joan naiz
      gone am
      c. etorri naiz
      come am

The following ones, on the contrary, are transitive forms:

(69)   a. eduki dut
           had have
       b. eraman dut
           taken have
       c. ekarri dut
           brought have

As can be observed, intransitive verbs, such as *egon* "to be," *joan* "to go," or *etorri* "to come," select the auxiliary *to be*, whereas transitive verbs, such as *eduki* "to have," *eraman* "to take," and *ekarri* "to bring," select *to have*. Selecting one or the other auxiliary based on the type of verb (or better said, predicate) is common in many languages such as French, German, Italian, and Dutch. We cannot go into the details of the reasoning behind this alternation, but it is convenient to know that not all languages select one or the other auxiliary based on the transitivity of the verb. There are more complicated languages in this respect, such as certain Italian dialects and Neapolitan in particular. Neapolitan selects *to have* when the subject is conjugated in the third person but instead selects *to be* when the subject is conjugated in the first or second person. Generally, in nondialectal Italian, however, auxiliary selection is based on the transitivity of the verb:

(70)   a. sono arrivato
           am arrived
       b. ho mangiato
           have eaten

As can be seen in (70a), the auxiliary *essere* "to be" has been selected, as the lexical verb (*arrivare* "to arrive") is intransitive. In (70b), on the other hand, the selected auxiliary is *avere* "to have" because the lexical verb (*mangiare* "to eat") is transitive.

It is worth noticing that Basque also exhibits internal variation regarding auxiliary selection: certain intransitive verbs, such as action verbs, take the intransitive auxiliary *izan* "to be" or the transitive auxiliary **edun* "to have" to express the same meaning depending on the variety. Let's take, for instance, the verb *jolastu* "to play." In *jolastu da* "she/he has played," the verb takes the intransitive auxiliary whereas in *jolastu du,* the verb takes the transitive auxiliary. Both instances have the same meaning, "she/he has played," but they take different auxiliary verbs depending on the variety.

As we can see, even if Basque is not a Romance language, it is surprisingly similar to some Romance languages in this respect. Whether the language is pre-Indo-European, like Basque, or Indo-European, like Italian and other Romance languages, does not seem to make much of a difference here. We are sorry to disappoint Basque speakers who, though they may not brag about the magnificence of this minority language, might occasionally brag about its ancestral idiosyncrasy and exoticism.

PARTICIPLES ACCOMPANIED BY AUXILIARIES

There is another not at all banal matter that Basque, English, and many other languages share, which is the fact that the auxiliary accompanies a verb in participle form. Readers can go back to the examples that we have given to verify this point. The truth is that, as we can see, Basque has its own exceptions, like all languages do, but we can say that an auxiliary will most likely be found next to a participle form. What is curious and has not been explained yet (although it is not unexplainable) is why the use of the participle is expanded to not only the present perfect (and other tenses), like in many other languages, but also to each and every one of the conjugated forms of those verbs without synthetic forms (such as *to be, to go, to bring, to take,* etc.). Thus, for instance, with a verb without synthetic forms such as *jan* "to eat," we say:

(71)   a. jan dut
        (I) have eaten
        b. jaten dut
        (I) am eating/(I) eat habitually
        c. jango dut
        (I) will eat/(I) am going to eat

All these forms include a participle, be it a perfective participle (*jan* "to eat"), an imperfective participle (*jaten* "eating"), or a future participle (*jango* "will eat"). And even more so, leaving aside some differences that will later be explained, exceptional linguistics scholars such as Koldo Mitxelena, about whom we will say more later, have appreciated the great similarities that Basque and other western European languages in this field. Remembering Mitxelena's words is never in vain:

> The analytic forms of the verb, what we also call periphrastic forms, share some similarities in both the perfectum and the future: *etorri da, egin du, est venu, ist gekommen (ant. is come)/has done, a fait, hat gemacht; joanen, joango da, lit.* "is to go," *eginen, egingo du* "has to do." (Mitxelena 1981 [2011]: 533).

It is fascinating to verify that the future forms in Basque are formed from a perfective participle form, such as *jan*, to which the genitive mark -(*r*)*en* is added in northeastern dialects and -*ko* (or -*go*) in southwestern dialects:

(72)   a. janen dut
      eaten have
      "have to eat"
      (according to Mitxelena's translation)
      (northeastern dialects)
      "(I) will eat"/"(I) am going to eat"

      b. jango dut
      eaten have
      "have to eat"
      (southeastern dialects)
      "(I) will eat"/"(I) am going to eat"

Oftentimes, rivers converge.

APPENDIX

The quote from Koldo Mitxelena's work was extracted from the 1981 article "Lengua común y dialectos vascos" ("Common Language and Basque Dialects"), published in *Palabras y textos*, pages 35–55. The article was again published in 2011 by Joseba A. Lakarra and Iñigo Ruiz Arzalluz in *Luis Michelena. Obras Completas. VII. Fonética y Fonología, Morfosintaxis y Dialectología*, pages 517–54.

Wonder Woman is an American superhero film directed by Patty Jenkins and distributed by Warner Bros. in 2017. Israeli actress Gal Gadot plays the role of Diana, the Amazonian warrior.

On Golden Pond is a 1981 drama directed by Mark Rydell starring Katharine Hepburn and Henry Fonda, with Jane Fonda in a supporting role. Hepburn and Henry Fonda received the Best Actress and Best Actor, respectively, in the fifty-fourth Academy Awards.

Loreak (Flowers) is a 2014 drama filmed in Basque and directed by Jon Garaño and Jose Mari Goenaga. Actresses Itziar Aizpuru, Itziar Ituño, and Nagore Aranburu play the three main roles.

5

The Strange Case of the Ergative

Subjects, objects, clothing, and case marking. Familiar subjects and recognizable objects. Don't try to trick Holmes. The strange case of the ergative. Ergative languages, eccentricities of nature. Insisting on my mistake. About Watson (and the absolutive case).

SUBJECTS, OBJECTS, CLOTHING, AND CASE MARKING

The previous chapter explored the nuances of Basque verbal inflection, and we mentioned that the protagonists of the event are explicitly expressed in the conjugated forms of the verb. Readers will recall that these protagonists are the subject, the direct object, and the indirect object. This chapter, however, only focuses on the first two, since the third one is not related to the present topic.

The path we took in the previous chapter to get to subjects and objects is, however, the inverse of the path usually taken by linguists handling this issue. Frequently, when linguists and grammarians talk about subjects and objects, they refer to instances, without necessarily considering verbal inflection, such as:

(73)   a. Sherlock Holmes lived at 221B Baker Street
        b. Sherlock Holmes examined the letter carefully

In the first sentence, Sherlock Holmes is the subject (who lived in an imaginary flat 221B on Baker Street)—we should recall that the intransitive verb "to live" leads to stories of only one protagonist. In (b) Sherlock Holmes is also the subject, but additionally, he examines a specific thing, the letter, which is the direct object—in this case, the verb "to examine" is transitive, and therefore, both Sherlock and the letter are the protagonists. Thus, Sherlock Holmes is the subject of both sentences, and the letter is the direct object of the second one. The first sentence, in this case, has no object. From now on, and unless stated otherwise, we will journey on this well-traveled path to discuss subjects and objects, and we will refer to syntactic constituents, such as "Sherlock Holmes" and "the letter" without stopping to consider verbal inflection for the time being.

The fact that subjects and objects exist in languages is not exclusive to English, Basque, or any other specific language of which readers might think. It is an inherent feature of any natural language simply because they are languages, which is totally understandable when we take into account that there is no good story without protagonists. Even those (French) movies that Woody Allen says are like watching grass grow, usually have a protagonist (beyond the grass, obviously).

What is interesting is not so much that languages have subjects and objects, or that these languages tell more or less intriguing stories about them. Rather, what is curious is that these subjects and objects appear with specific clothing that makes them easily identifiable to speakers. For instance, we cannot help but recall the famous detective from our examples with the hunting cap (called deerstalker), which has front and back visors that cover the face and neck, and two earflaps that are tied on top. This hunting cap, which Sidney Paget mistakenly used in an illustration in the short story "The Boscombe Valley Mystery" (from The Adventures of Sherlock Holmes, Arthur Conan Doyle, 1891) and substituting the original cloth cap, became our beloved character's identity trademark. In addition to this hunting cap, Sherlock Holmes is also recognized for his meerschaum (seafoam, in German) pipe that actually owes its suggestive name to the mineral sepiolite from which it is made. It is also not true that the pipe belonged to the imagination of Doyle, but rather it became popular, from the end of the nineteenth century onward, thanks to William Gillette's interpretation of the detective on a theater stage. Mistake or not, original or re-created, both the hunting cap and the curved pipe remind us of the memorable detective, without forgetting his tweed, of course. This attire has undoubtedly evolved throughout history: Basil Rathbone's tweed in the American classic movies of the mid-twentieth century was replaced by an elegant Milford coat made of pure Irish wool, worn by the brilliant Benedict Cumberbatch in the excellent BBC Sherlock series. None of this presents an obstacle that prevents the essential identity trademarks of our hero to endure. Elementary, my dear Watson.

I elaborated so much on Holmes that I am running out of ink for Watson. Since he is used to going unnoticed and does not normally attract as much attention as his colleague, I guess he will also forgive me. Anyway, each of them has his own clothing and personality, and both are otherwise unmistakable.

Again, languages are in some aspects more constrained and discreet than the wonderful characters created by such powerful minds as Doyle and re-created by illustrators, designers, and actors in one way or another. What is fundamental is that subjects and objects dress each in their own way, while both dressing in unique ways. Maybe it is not the tweed and the hunting cap accompanied by a seafoam pipe but only an apparently less elaborate costume that linguists call *case*.

FAMILIAR SUBJECTS AND RECOGNIZABLE OBJECTS

Case marks the arguments of the sentence in a particular way. It is true that sometimes we do not appreciate this mark because it is precisely characterized by its absence. This absence, however, would not hinder the mind of a man of reason, such as Holmes. The only two examples from this chapter are once again mentioned below:

(74) a. Sherlock Holmes lived at 221B Baker Street
   b. Sherlock Holmes examined the letter carefully

As discussed above, Sherlock Holmes is the subject of both sentences where all morphological marking for identification is absent. What seems undeniable—and Holmes himself would immediately recognize this—is that this unmarked subject is always identical in English, and it does not seem to care much about whether it takes an intransitive verb (like "to live") or a transitive one (like "to examine").

Someone such as Holmes, however, would not be satisfied with the most immediate evidence. He would probably compare it to other pieces of evidence to prove that this evidence indeed points to one irrefutable fact: all subjects are marked in the same way or, rather, are unmarked in the same way. It is likely that he then would think about other languages such as Spanish, which would provide new evidence to compare with English. He would come up with sentences such as these:

(75)   a. Sherlock Holmes vivía en el 221B de Baker Street
          Sherlock Holmes lived at 221B of Baker Street
       b. Sherlock Holmes analizó la carta con detenimiento
          Sherlock Holmes examined the letter with care

He might even continue with the same method and suggest complementing his sample with other languages that could provide new evidence to confirm or reject his particular truth about subject marking. Now, suppose that he considered a language from a bygone era that was well known to him. He might then recall his knowledge of Latin and create a sentence like:

(76)   a. Latin: *Magistra venit*
          Spanish: *La maestra viene*
          "The teacher is coming"
       b. Latin: *Magistra puellam videt*
          Spanish: *La maestra ve a la niña*
          "The teacher sees the girl"

Much like in the corresponding English and Spanish sentences, the subject *magistra* "teacher" is also identical in both sentences, even though they contain opposing verbs: intransitive (*venio, venire* ... "to come" or *venir* in Spanish) in the first sentence and transitive (*video, videre* ... "to see" or *ver* in Spanish) in the second. Once again, Holmes would only confirm that he was right, since every subject is marked in the same way, independent of the language.

Holmes would probably not stop there either, as that would be too boring. He would certainly also look at the object in the transitive phrase to confirm its form. Furthermore, it is more than likely that he would turn things around and put *magistra* "teacher" in the object position and *puella* "girl" in the place of the subject, in which case, he would get:

(77)   a. Puella venit
       b. Puella magistram videt

He would thus confirm that indeed not only are subjects marked alike, but when they switch positions and appear as objects, then their form changes: if *girl* appears in the subject position, then it is *puella*; on the contrary, if *girl* appears in an object position, then it is *puellam*. If something similar happens with *teacher*, then it is *magistra* in the subject position and *magistram* in the object position. Precisely the form that *children* and *teachers* take in Holmes' eyes is because of the particular clothing of subjects and objects that we discussed before. The case of *puella* is known as the *nominative* case and that of *puellam* is known as the *accusative* case. Languages like Latin that differentiate subject and object marking are known among academics as nominative-accusative languages or simply accusative languages. English, Spanish, French, and other Romance languages, many but not all other Indo-European languages, and even some non-Indo-European languages such as Miskito on the Atlantic coast of Nicaragua share this property.

DON'T TRY TO TRICK HOLMES

Inflectional marking of subject and object, which in Latin is morphologically transparent, is not so apparent in languages such as English, Spanish, and French. In Spanish and French, time has worn down the case endings that were present in Latin. In Old English as well, nouns had different endings depending on their function in the sentence, but these endings have also been eroded. Thus, the morphological features that are so clearly marked in a language such as Latin are significantly less evident to the senses in other languages, and these features must be reconstructed by tracing back morphological features here and there, which Holmes would be perfectly capable of interpreting (even though the question would of course be how). This morphological distinction between certain subjects and objects is not as evident in English, French, or Spanish as it is in Latin. Consider for example:

(78)   a. Sherlock saw Watson
        b. Watson saw Sherlock

Sherlock is identical in both subject and object positions, and the same thing happens with Watson when he sees or when he is seen. A man of logic would merely note that the way in which subjects and objects are marked in English is not the same as in Latin. Nonetheless, they might be surprised to discover that regarding pronouns, the difference between subjects and objects seems indeed real.

(79)   a. He went home
        b. He saw her
        c. She saw him

Hence, a third-person masculine pronoun has the form *he* in the subject position but takes the form *him* when in the object position. Something similar happens with *she*, its feminine counterpart, since it is *she* for the subject and *her* for the object. Of course, this change in form results from case marking, which marks pronouns with different cases when they appear in different syntactic positions (subject or object). In other words, *he* is not only third-person singular and masculine but also bears the nominative case (subject case). The same applies to *him*, which bears the accusative case (object case). As illustrated below, these forms are not at all interchangeable: a pronoun in the accusative case cannot occupy the subject position (a, b, c), and a pronoun in the nominative case cannot occupy the object position (d, e).

(80)　a. *Him went home
　　　b. *Him saw her
　　　c. *Her saw him
　　　d. *He saw she
　　　e. *She saw he

At this point, Holmes should decide how to interpret the data in (78) above, in which neither Sherlock nor Watson is morphologically distinguished as subject or object; that is, through morphological case marking. Obviously, we do not know for sure how he would approach the challenge. It is likely that he would assume that the case and pronoun systems in a language are not the same, as many inductivist typologists agree today. However, it might be the case that, even being a man of logic as he is, he might be persuaded by deduction and might conclude that the objects Watson and Sherlock are marked in an abstract way. These objects would not be marked with an overt morphological case, as in Latin, or as pronouns are in English, but rather with an abstract accusative case. This idea is essential to understand the case system in English and whether it is similar to the Latin system. In any case, nobody, neither Holmes nor anybody else, would doubt that English has other syntactic mechanisms, such as word order, that undoubtedly allow us to refer to subjects, objects, and their great asymmetry. Except for some differences (small differences for deductivists and not so small for Holmesian or Sherlockian inductivists), Spanish is similar to English, and Holmes is not expected to be too surprised. The mystery, however, is hidden not too far from the house number on Baker Street.

THE STRANGE CASE OF THE ERGATIVE

Linguistics, just like speakers, sometimes becomes a little ethno-centric, thinking that many of the basic characteristics of natural languages are those of European languages and, more specifically, those of a handful of them. After all, linguistics is the work of linguists who are human and, therefore, cannot simply be exempt from the weaknesses to which humans are subject.

More often than not, what we think is true is only true up to the crucial point where it is not true anymore. This is what would happen if this chapter were finished at this point, after analyz-ing in more or less detail some languages to which the field of linguistics has devoted special attention throughout its history.

Let's come back to Holmes and his method. For him, the starting sample is crucial, and in this sample, languages such as the ones previously analyzed in this chapter would allow him to advance a certain truth, even if only a provisional truth. Nonetheless, even before starting to analyze the sample, Holmes would consider all logical possibilities that could exist to mark subjects and objects. In all probability, not only would he notice the possibility that all subjects are marked the same way with one case, but there could also exist the potential that, unlike objects, not all subjects need be marked in the same way. The sample analyzed so far shows that this logical possi-bility is not attested to, but this could be because of the nature of the sample size and not so much to the actual absence of this logical possibility.

Let's assume that Holmes extended his study to Basque, a lesser-known and less-studied language at that time, even if a number of works had already been published by Louis-Lucien Bonaparte, Napoleon's famous nephew and a fundamental pillar of classic Basque dialectology. We cannot but imagine that Holmes, a man educated in prestigious universities such as Oxford and Cambridge, was well aware of the existence of minority languages such as Basque. Even given the likelihood that he studied French and German—but never Basque—at

those universities, and even if he had no clue about the existence of Basque despite his education, he lived in Bordeaux
and Pau, France, as a child, which are very close to the Basque
Country. Therefore, it can be assumed that he had probably heard
of Basque. If not him, then perhaps Watson, who many consider to be Conan Doyle's alter ego (and who incidentally was
Scottish) knew something of it. One way or another, let's assume
he included Basque in his sample. He would find the following
sentences, previously analyzed in English and Spanish:

(81)   a. Sherlock Holmes Baker Street-eko 221B-n bizi zen
        b. Sherlock Holmesek gutuna aztertu zuen arretaz

These two sentences and their previous equivalents have the
same subject: Sherlock Holmes. The subject of the first sentence
has no identifying mark. That is to say, it is unmarked, like in
English and Spanish. In the second sentence, however, Sherlock
examines "a letter" (*gutuna*) "carefully" (*arretaz*). This is, therefore,
a transitive sentence. The subject of this second sentence carries
an unexpected mark, *-(e)k*, so the subject, in this case, is marked.
This unexpected marking seems to contradict the truth we have
accepted thus far: all subjects are marked in the same way and
with the same case. Hence, considering the evidence, Holmes
would encounter the strange case of *-(e)k*, marking Sherlock
Holmes in the second sentence, contrary to his expectations. He
would then try to identify this marker in other simple sentences
(without adjuncts), which might allow him to see it more clearly,
if possible. Let's go back to the previous sentences in Latin and
look for their equivalents in Basque:

(82)   a. Andereñoa dator
           the teacher is coming
        b. Andereñoak neskatoa ikusi du
           the teacher girl seen has

Holmes would then, move "the girl" (*neskatoa*) to subject
position and "the teacher" (*andereñoa*) to object position:

(83)   a. Neskatoa dator
         the girl comes
         b. Neskatoak andereñoa ikusi du
         the girl the teacher seen has

Then he would indeed confirm that there is the same case
ending (-*k* in this case and not -*(e)k*, since a vowel corresponding to the determiner -*a* is added), which marks the subject in
transitive sentences.

He would even create transitive sentences, where the subject
lacks the case marking -*k*, to reaffirm its status and relevance. He
would then notice that that would produce ungrammatical sentences, such as the following:

(84)   a. *Andereñoa neskatoa ikusi du
         the teacher the girl seen has
         b. *Neskatoa andereñoa ikusi du
         the girl the teacher seen has

To continue experimenting, Holmes should use the same
subject marking with intransitive sentences. He would then
observe that the -*k* mark is added to subjects of transitive but
not intransitive sentences. If the -*k* is added to the subject of an
intransitive sentence, the sentence is defective:

(85)   a. *Andereñoak dator
         the teacher comes
         b. *Neskatoak dator
         the girl comes

Thus, Holmes would conclude by saying that a strange case,
absent in English, Latin, and Spanish, manifests in Basque.
Despite his knowledge, what Holmes would not know is that this
strange case had already been discovered by a certain Fabricius
who, in a study on Greenlandic Inuit, called it *nominativus transi-*
tivus, using the name *nominativus intransitivus* for the corresponding (unmarked) case of an intransitive subject. Anyhow, the name

that now is commonly used for this case marking is ergative (from Greek *ergon* "work"). This term was established by Adolf Dirr, a linguist and ethnologist who wrote a description of Rutul in 1921. Rutul is a northeastern Caucasian language that, like Basque and Greenlandic, has this ergative case (and its unmarked alter ego known as absolutive case). However, that was only two years before we completely lost our detective's track, which makes us suspect that he left the strange case of the ergative unsolved.

ERGATIVE LANGUAGES, ECCENTRICITIES OF NATURE

A language with an ergative case system, such as Basque, would have posed a great challenge for the analytic mind of a detective with an accusative mind such as Holmes. Surely he would have enjoyed the challenge! Let's revisit some of the data analyzed in this chapter to study some the key pieces of this challenge.

Evidently, one of the keys is the presence in transitive sentences like (86b, c) of the strange ergative case discussed in this chapter. Its appearance is surprising because certain subjects in (86b, c) are marked but others like in (86a) are not. Moreover, the story does not end here. Leaving the ergative aside for a moment, if we examine a different case, the absolutive, which is unmarked and more low profile (kind of a Watson turned into a case), readers will notice that this case is not only assigned (that's how it's said) to the subject of the intransitive sentence in (86a) but also to the object in (86b, c).

(86)   a. Andereñoa dator
          the teacher comes
       b. Andereñoak neskatoa ikusi du
          the teacher the girl seen has
       c. Neskatoak andereñoa ikusi du
          the girl the teacher seen has

Thus, *andereñoa* ("the teacher") is in the absolutive case in both the subject position of the intransitive sentence (86a) and in the object position of the transitive sentence in (86c). In the eyes of a speaker of an accusative language, where two very differentiated functions, such as subject and object, are each marked with a different case and are never mixed in any way, the case marking that we find in Basque is an eccentricity of nature in the best of cases. For many speakers, it is intolerable, and some of them would even rush to correct you. Of course, that would not be the case with Holmes, who would smile. He would light his pipe with his atavistic gesture and conceal his surprise. At the end of the day, his mind already contemplated the logical possibility that a language of this nature existed, so it would not be too crazy to finally discover one.

Biological eccentricities such as this are not extensively seen in Europe, where the map is mainly accusative. The previously mentioned description of Rutul, a language spoken in the Republic of Dagestan in Russia with a population of thirty thousand speakers, however, popularized the term ergative. Many other Caucasian languages are of ergative nature, and while it is true that it is a geographical area between eastern Europe and western Asia, it is also true that many of those languages, such as Georgian or Kartvelian, are spoken in Europe as well as Asia. More than one researcher has proposed a genetic relationship between Basque and Caucasian languages, among others. That many of these languages are ergative like Basque, despite their geographic diversity, is probably not insignificant. In any case, this matter is in expert hands. As I mentioned, I am one of those people who does not become obsessed over supposed language orphanhood. At the end of the day, Basque is just another natural language that has more or less, in the eyes of a stranger (but not mine), extravagant characteristics that are however also attested in other languages, which are not necessarily immediate family or closest neighbors. Holmes would share this opinion.

Another ergative language family is the Berber language family, which includes Tamazight and the already extinct Guanche languages formerly spoken in the Canary Islands. Some linguists have stubbornly sought a genetic relationship between Basque, Berber, and the Caucasian languages. As far as I know, on the other hand, Basque has not been linked to other ergative languages, such as Burushaski (a genetically isolate language of Pakistan), the Eskimo-Aleut languages, or the Mayan languages. It might just be a matter of time though. All in all, this might explain the eccentric natures of Basque and Burushaski, the Basque people's admiration for the Himalayas, and Martin Zabaleta's great achievement, as the first Basque mountaineer to leave tracks on the summit of Everest with his Sherpa Pasang Temba in the legendary 1980 expedition that we will never forget. Or, if Basque is related to Tzotzil and Tzeltal, that might explain the presence of evidence of Basque-like Pelota sports in Mayan ruins, as well as the great accomplishments of some of the best Basque Pelota sportsmen in history, such as Julián Retegi. Concerning Chucoto, a Chucoto-Kamchatka family language and the Inuit language of Greenland, or the Aboriginal languages of Australia, again, it might just be a matter of time.

INSISTING ON MY MISTAKE

After reflecting upon the eccentricities of Basque, someone such as Holmes, who is also an eccentric, could not but sympathize with the language, without even trying to put it in its proper place. It is questionable whether his cocaine addiction increased or not because of his more cinematographic alter ego. This addiction, together with his passion for boxing, which is difficult to reconcile with his passion for Stradivarius, his interest in apiculture, and other more intrinsic features of his nature such as his arrogance and misogyny, play an essential part of his idiosyncrasy, without which it would be difficult to understand his character.

Now we need to ask readers to remember some of the previously discussed issues regarding verbal inflection. In particular, we need to recall what we learned about subjects and objects, but now we must also consider conjugated verb forms. The question is basically this: if a language such as Basque distinguishes transitive and intransitive subjects through the ergative and absolutive case respectively, then how are subjects expressed in the realm of verbal inflection? Does Basque have one or two forms for subjects? Well, being acutely aware of the consequences of his own extravagance and as insistent on his mistakes as Basque speakers are, Holmes would have no doubt about it: of course, there are two different forms. And he is quite right.

We shall consider some examples and add something that was omitted up until now in order to not bother readers with terminological matters that are crucial for experts but unnecessary if we want to allow for the flow of our most intimate and intuitive knowledge about the universe and, therefore, languages.

Subjects and objects have been discussed on two separate occasions in this book. First, in the previous chapter, when verbal inflection was discussed, second, in this chapter, when learning how to mark Sherlock Holmes and company in the sentence, as well as when introducing the notion of case. However, strictly speaking, when we speak of subjects and objects we refer to these elements (Sherlock, etc.), whereas when we talk about verbal inflection we refer to subject and object agreement markers. That being said and returning to the examples, not only argument (subjects and objects) marking and case (ergative or absolutive) need to be analyzed in this instance, but their corresponding agreement markers in the verbal form also need to be analyzed.

(87)   a. Ni etorri **na**iz
          I come have
          "I have come"
        b. Zuk ni ikusi **na**uzu
          you I seen have
          "You have seen me"
        c. Nik zu ikusi zai**tu**t
          I you seen have
          "I have seen you"

Let's go step by step. In the first sentence (87a), the subject *ni* "I" is marked in the absolutive case, as it is also in sentence (b), where this word is in object position. On the other hand, *ni* "I" is the subject in the transitive sentence (c), and it carries the strange ergative mark -*k*, previously mentioned in the chapter.

Let's observe the verb forms and see how the agreement system is articulated. When the sentence is intransitive (87a) and the subject is, therefore, absolutive (*ni* "I"), the agreement marker is *na*. However, when the sentence is transitive (c) and the subject is, consequently, ergative (*nik* "I"), the agreement marker for this subject is not the *na* preceding the root, but it is the *t* following it. Thus, the same agreement marker cannot be attributed to both subjects. On the other hand, when the first-person singular pronoun is the object of the sentence (b), then the agreement marker is the same for that pronoun as for the intransitive subject (a), which is *na*. In short, even if the case system were very clear, the agreement system confirms the facts (subjects fall into two different types, and objects are marked like intransitive subjects), in case any skeptic might have any doubts.

As a result, referring to subject and object agreement markers does not seem to be the most appropriate thing for Basque (nor other ergative languages), since there are not one but two types of subject agreement markers, and the marker corresponding to the subject of the intransitive sentence also corresponds to the object of the transitive sentence.

What is the same: the language, like Holmes and even ourselves, is absurdly and deliciously insistent on its mistakes.

ABOUT WATSON (AND THE ABSOLUTIVE CASE)

It is an undeniable fact that Holmes' analytical brilliance and his innate and almost superhuman ability for discovery has deprived Dr. Watson of any possibility of standing out. Dr. Watson, however, even without Holmes' qualities, has an excellent medical education and years of experience as a surgeon in the British Army. Even if he did not practice boxing, he used to play rugby. He is, with his Victorian demeanor, discretion, and humanity, the perfect counterpoint to an irresistible but unbearable Holmes.

The previous comparison between Watson and the absolutive is not trivial. Both Holmes and the ergative gained excessive fame, whereas Watson and the absolutive survived quietly and with difficulty in the background. However, we should not forget that Watson is an eternal narrator, the essential voice-over that has told us so many stories, and if he had narrated his own story, maybe the ergative would not fare as well.

The question is the following: if accusative languages have a clear asymmetry between subjects and objects, and that clear asymmetry is morphologically manifested through case (and agreement markers), then in ergative languages where subjects are not uniquely marked and some of them are marked as objects, should we think that there is not a clear distinction between subjects and objects?

The answer is no. That is to say, we do not speak of subjects and objects in ergative languages to give readers false hints and take them to a dead end. However, in particular constructions, the argument in the ergative case, or in other words, the argument that bears the marked case—the apparently strange, eccentric, exotic, and colorful case—is not the fundamental axis sustaining the syntactic pillars of the construction. This argument marked with the ergative case is vilified by the language's syntax, which, against all odds, prefers the less brilliant but consistent Watson with an exceptional moustache, and therefore, the absolutive case, whether it be intransitive subject or transitive object.

These constructions have been analyzed in detail in specialized literature, and in relevant cases, they imply the interpretation of what theoretical grammar refers to as *silent categories*. These silent categories, those that exist in syntax even though nobody hears or sees them, will be discussed next.

Suppose that you need to interpret one of these silent categories in English.

(88)   Holmes saw Dr. Watson and (ø) rushed to leave

This example illustrates a conjoined sentence consisting of two simple sentences coordinated by the conjunction *and*. The second clause (*and rushed to leave*) has an omitted subject, or in other words, a silent category that needs to be interpreted. No English speaker would have any doubts as to how to interpret this category. Everyone, without exception, would interpret that he who rushed to leave is Holmes, that is, the subject of the first clause and not Dr. Watson, the object of that same clause. That means that if there is a silent category and that category is the subject, then that (silent) subject inevitably traces back to another subject. Moreover, the other interpretation where Dr. Watson, and not Holmes, is who rushed to leave would undoubtedly be ungrammatical.

Let's look now at languages other than English, such as Dyirbal, an Australian language from North Queensland documented by Robert M. W. Dixon, a linguist who has studied ergative languages. Dixon provided an excellent description of the language, even though, according to Ethnologue's 2006 census, it had only twenty-nine speakers, which makes us think that without Holmes' brilliance, Dyirbal is about to die if it has not already gone extinct as I write these lines. Dyirbal's data will not be broached, but rather its abstract skeleton will be studied. The English example above will be taken as a starting point, and glosses will be added to guide our understanding of its corresponding Dyirbal. ERG is used for ergative and ABS for absolutive.

(89) Holmes.ERG saw Dr. Watson.ABS and (∅) rushed to leave

The first clause is a transitive sentence, and therefore, it has two protagonists, the subject and the object, which are marked with the ergative and accusative cases, respectively. The second clause, on the contrary, is an intransitive sentence. In Dyirbal, strictly speaking, there is no *and* conjunction. Instead, it is something like having one sentence next to the other, although in principle, this is not relevant for us to reflect upon. Readers may consult the bibliography, as Holmes would do, to delve deeper into this issue. What is relevant is that in our example there is a silent category, the subject of rushed to leave, that Dyirbal speakers need to interpret. The fact is that when these speakers interpret the silent category and consider both possibilities, Holmes (subject.erg) and Watson (object.abs), they not only interpret that Watson (the object of the first clause) rushed to leave, but furthermore, the other interpretation, where Holmes (the subject of the first clause) left, would be ungrammatical for them.

Things being as they are, it is understandable that many ergative languages prefer Watson to Holmes and choose the absolutive and not the ergative as their syntactic pivot when considering certain matters. Furthermore, if Holmes and his wounded ego claimed what is rightfully his, he would have to turn to one of his passions and disguise himself, or syntactically transform, to occupy the more prominent position of his colleague Dr. Watson.

In a language like this, the only chance for Holmes (the ergative) to be allowed to be taken into consideration as the subject of the second clause is to dress up as Watson (the absolutive). Languages are wise and actually do that. As it is Carnival time while I write these lines, they look in the closet for an absolutive disguise, as Holmes in (90b). This sentence is the carnivalesque intransitivized counterpart to the transitive sentence in (90a). This intransitivized construction is called *antipassive* and is marked by a morpheme also known as antipassive.

(90)   a. Holmes.ERG saw Dr. Watson.ABS
       b. Holmes.ABS saw.ANTIP Dr. Watson.DAT

In both sentences, Holmes sees Watson, while nothing remains the same. The carnivalesque antipassive, thanks to the antipassive morpheme, is intransitivized. As a result, one single argument (and protagonist) remains in the sentence. This argument is obviously Holmes, who is dressed up in absolutive case (that is, it opted for more modest clothing, and for this reason, it is more effective). Thanks to his boxing abilities and without further consideration, Holmes has thrown Watson to the canvas. Watson thus becomes a new resigned adjunct (marked in dative case, which will be explained later, or in its absence, another non-relevant oblique case). In this way, Holmes can get his indisputable authority back again. When the antipassive with Holmes dressed up in the absolutive is created, Dyirbal speakers have only one option to interpret the silent category that rushed to leave: of course, it is Holmes.

(91)   Holmes.ABS saw.ANTIP Dr. Watson.DAT and rushed to leave

When ergative languages behave in this syntactic manner, linguists refer to syntactic ergativity rather than to the previously mentioned morphological ergativity, which consists of morphologically manifesting ergativity through case and agreement.

Eventually, readers might wonder why we have not analyzed Basque data instead of the glossed English as Dyirbal. The answer is that, even if morphological ergativity in Basque is absolutely clear and extensively documented, with regard to the interpretation of silent categories in the contexts presented above, the minds of Basque speakers differ from those of Australian aboriginals and are more similar to their neighboring Spanish and French speakers' minds. Thus, for Basque speakers, the interpretation of the following sentence should be that Holmes (and not Watson) rushes to leave:

(92)   Holmes.ERG saw Dr. Watson.ABS and rushed to leave

The reason why Basque has no carnivalesque antipassives is difficult to determine, despite the fact that there is a well-known Carnival festival in a small Basque town named Tolosa. It is even more difficult to say why Basque differs from typologically homologue languages and looks more similar to neighboring non-typologically related ones. In any case, there are no problems without solutions, but there are ill-posed problems, as Holmes and even our dear Dr. Watson know very well.

APPENDIX

Sherlock Holmes and Dr. Watson are part of the popular imaginary and do not need to be introduced. Therefore, I abstain from referencing more than what I already have about them in the text. Of course, I take this opportunity to recommend their eternal reading.

Ergativity is maybe one of the typological phenomena in Basque that has received the most attention within Basque grammar, particularly since the 1990s. It is also a parameter about which linguists from different scientific traditions, be they formalist or functionalist, have carefully reflected. The literature is so extensive that only one piece of work will be cited, a book that is like the Bible in the field of syntactic variation. This book is *Ergativity* by Robert M. W. Dixon, published by Cambridge University Press in 1994. Regarding ergativity in Basque, a number of studies by Itziar Laka are especially relevant, for instance, "Unergatives that assign ergative, unaccusatives that assign accusative," published by Jonathan D. Bobaljik and Colin Phillips in *Papers on Case and Agreement I* [WITWPL 18], pages 149–172. Another recent article on the topic is "Ergativity in Basque," coauthored by Ane Berro and Ricardo Etxepare and published by Jessica Coon, Diane Massam, and Lisa Travis in the *Handbook of Ergativity* (Oxford University Press, pages 782–806).

The references to both Fabricius and Adolf Dirr have been extracted from Dixon's book. Those of you willing to delve deeper into more technical issues can search for *The World Atlas of Language Structures* online [http://wals.info/], edited by the well-known typologists Matthew S. Dryer and Martin Haspelmath. It contains a chapter on antipassives written by Maria Polinsky [http://wals.info/chapter/108] titled Antipassive Constructions.

6

There is Strength in Numbers

There is strength in numbers. We speak the same language. Visionary statesmen and a declaration of principles. Making decisions. Long-term memory.

THERE IS STRENGTH IN NUMBERS

The unification of the Basque language was an arduous and complicated process. However, we will not go over it, because this great story has already been told on numerous occasions by the dialectologist Koldo Zuazo, among others, not only in his doctoral thesis—which was entirely written in Basque—but also in his book *Standard Basque and its Dialects*, in case readers want to indulge their curiosity.

When I revisit that fascinating but equally winding story, a Basque proverb comes to mind: *zenbat buru, hainbat aburu* "so many men, so many minds." When readers recite this proverb—which I know they will, and I appreciate and applaud their efforts—they should try to pronounce it with the s in *sun*, with the back of their tongues. The tongue moves forward in the alveolar region of the mouth, which, in case readers do not know, is the region located at the back of their superior teeth. On the other hand, the *h* is silent for many Basque speakers, and, unlike in English, the *h* in *hainbat* does not need to be aspirated. However, it does need to be written in to avoid orthographic errors. This *h* was not without controversy in the normativization of Basque, and while it is difficult to resist the temptation,

I will not discuss this issue. If interested, readers can find the details in Zuazo's work. In this chapter, I will not discuss the *h*, but I will discuss the aspects involved in the unification and nor-mativization of the Basque language, especially its morphology (and in a sense, its syntax). I will neither explain the milestones of the Basque unification process nor the nature of the propos-als or arguments put forth by different authors. Ultimately, this is a grammar book and not a historical language normalization book. Nonetheless, I cannot help but discuss the creation of *eus-kara batua*, that is, unified or standard Basque, because, in spite of many differences in opinion—some of them triggering extremely heated discussions—for once, there was agreement, and agree-ment resulted in unity.

I rescued the proverb *so many men, so many minds* from obliv-ion, which, not being gender inclusive, many think should be kept in disuse. I have no doubts though about the fact that read-ers are very familiar with another popular phrase that perfectly encompasses the great story of the normativization of Basque: *there is strength in numbers.*

WE SPEAK THE SAME LANGUAGE

It may seem obvious, but before discussing Basque dialects, it is nec-essary to revisit the premise of this book: even two apparently very different languages such as Basque and English are actually very similar. Based on this assumption, which is also the initial thesis of this book, when getting into the study of not language but dialectal variation, this thesis can only be corroborated. Dialects might appar-ently seem very different, like when comparing western Basque dia-lects to central Basque dialects or when comparing these dialects to Souletin Basque dialects, etc., but they are undoubtedly similar.

Basque dialects currently share several characteristics, having shared even more in the past. As many experts have shown, time, among other factors, ended up acting as a scattering force that resulted in distancing these dialects when, in the past, they were not so far apart.

Among the several characteristics shared by Basque dialects, some have already been discussed in this book and attributed to language in general, and others will be mentioned for the first time in this chapter. Throughout the book, I do not at all pretend to be exhaustive, but instead I aim to provide some pieces of the puzzle that might help readers disentangle intricate aspects of Basque, its varieties, and eventually language itself, which is simultaneously subject to universal principles and variation parameters.

Some of the characteristics already well known to our readers are, for instance, that all Basque dialects are ergative. That is, all Basque dialects mark the subject with the ergative case (*k*) and mark the object with the absolutive case in transitive sentences, as well as the subject of intransitive sentences. All Basque dialects have a dative case (*i*) that marks indirect objects, among others. With certain verbs, all Basque dialects have synthetic verb forms, such as *nator* "I come" or *dakart* "I bring it," and they all have analytic verb forms that combine the verb in participle form with an auxiliary verb, such as *etorri naiz* "I have come" or *ekarri dut* "I have brought it." All Basque dialects have at least two auxiliary verbs—*izan* "to be" and *edun* "to have"—that are roughly and respectively combined with transitive and intransitive verbs (*etorri naiz* translated as "come I-am" and *ekarri dut* as "brought it-have-I"). Verbal inflection contains ergative, absolutive, and dative agreement markers, such as in *ekarri dizut* "brought it-to-you-have-I" in each and every Basque dialect.

There are also many other common characteristics. For example, all Basque dialects have postpositions that roughly correspond to prepositions in English (some have already been mentioned). All Basque dialects express tense (past or present), aspect (perfective or imperfective), and mode (indicative, subjective, or imperative) in conjugated verb forms. And of course, all Basque dialects have coordination and subordination mechanisms.

All these common characteristics of Basque dialects are essential to the language and characterize Basque in a peculiar manner within a complex typological universe: for instance, whether it is ergative and not accusative, whether it alternates the auxiliaries *to be* and *to have*, and whether it allows null subjects, direct and indirect objects, etc. If these typological characteristics were to be listed, one could see that all dialects share a very large number of them (we challenge the most skeptical readers to draft a hypothetical list and engineers to quantify them). Nonetheless, even within these common characteristics, we can observe morphological variation, which can distort the most solid principles of a universalist such as myself. For example, in Lauaxeta's poem *Itauna* "The Question," written in the western or Bizkaian dialect, (a) corresponds exactly to (b), in standard Basque:

(93)   a. Itaundu dautsozu "You have asked him/her"
       b. Galdetu diozu

In the first place, between (a) and (b), there is a lexical difference (*itaundu* vs. *galdetu*), which in both cases means "to ask." We do not deny it; they are definitely very different words. We will not address lexical matters as much as morphological and syntactic aspects here, which is the primary focus of this book (without diminishing the crucial importance of lexical or other phonetic or phonological matters in the characterization of Basque dialects and Basque; just to give an example, Basque has more than ten different words to refer to the language: *euskara, euskera, euzkera, eskuara, eskuera, eskara, eskera, eskoara, euskiera, auskera, uskara, oskara, uskera, uskaa,* and *uska*). If we focus on the similarities, we observe the suffix *tu* in *galdetu* "to ask" (or *du* after the nasal consonant *n* in *itaundu*, also meaning "to ask"), which is associated with the perfective participle (and is also the form that dictionaries use to catalog these verbs). Let's take a second, however, to look at the auxiliary form, that is, the western form *dautsozu* and its central correlate *diozu*, which we have already analyzed in detail. Indeed, both forms appear with ditransitive verbs such as "to give" (in our example "to ask"), both forms are tripersonal forms ("to-him/her-it-you-have"), and in both forms, agreement markers align one after another in the same way. There are two differences though: the first is that in the western form *dautsozu,* the dative agreement marker is preceded by the preposition *ts,* whereas in its corresponding central form *diozu,* the agreement marker is preceded by *i;* the second difference is that in the form *dautsozu,* the root of the auxiliary "to have" (*u*) appears morphologically, while in its corresponding form *diozu,* it does not (even if we assume that this root exists). As a result of these differences, both forms are morphologically distinct, even though they are generated by a common syntactic mechanism. In fact, one of the great questions that needed to be resolved during the arduous Basque unification process was which form should be the dialectal basis of the multiple auxiliaries, among which tripersonal forms exist. That is, these experts had to decide whether western forms such as *dautsozu,* central forms such as *diozu,* or any other would be the basis of tripersonal forms.

    It all happened at the Baiona Congress in August 1964, a crucial month during an even more crucial year when not only *euskara batua* was born but also the author of this book. Standard Basque was born on August 29, 1964, seven days before the author herself.

    Koldo Zuazo and Pello Salaburu, among others, tell us that this congress was the result of the work of an organization created in Baiona in 1963 called *Euskal Idazkaritza* "Basque Secretariat." It also oversaw a Language Section (Idazkaritza'ko Hizkuntza Sailla) formed by representatives of Basque society, among whom José Luis Álvarez Enparantza "Txillardegi" stood out most. The *Agreements of the Baiona Congress* (*Baiona'ko Biltzarraren Erabakiak*) were published in the well-known journal *Jakin* in issue number 18 of 1965, pages 20–28.

    I will review linguistic matters shortly, although not so much those gathered in the resolutions adopted at that congress—even if they were only a few crucial points—but rather, the linguistic matters that little by little came to configure the nature of standard Basque in its current form. For now, I want to review a brief note from *Jakin*'s advisory board, which precedes the publication of the resolutions and reflects the spirit of those that were directly involved in the production of the Basque language. The translated text reads:

The Basque Secretariat of Baiona has done a great job. They have taken a fundamental step towards the unification of Basque literature. It was essential. Was it a good or bad step?

We cannot judge. In any case, *Jakin* approved all these decisions and will abide by them. Therefore, from now on, from our next issue onward, these rules will be mandatory in *Jakin*.

In *Jakin*, anyone can write in any dialect or style. But *Jakin* will abide by what the Basque Secretariat suggests, and for that reason, articles *Jakin* receives must follow those rules. Therefore, whoever wants to publish in our journal *Jakin* will be compelled to follow these rules.

From now on, whether authors follow these rules or not, in the case that articles are submitted without following these rules, the board of the journal *Jakin* will correct them.

The advisory board's note emphasized the importance of those resolutions and, without judging them, they agreed to abide by those resolutions without exception from that issue forward, even correcting received articles if deemed necessary. Without their involvement, as well as that of many other social agents, like writers, journalists, *andereños* from *ikastolas*, and translators, those resolutions would have served little purpose. To some of these pioneers, we owe thanks for their dedication, courage, and brilliance in the design and creation of standard Basque. To others, we are indebted for their willingness to make a commitment in using, transmitting, and disseminating standard Basque. All of them made it possible for standard Basque to be one language, as it had always been and still is, after long dialectal fragmentation. It is a language that, despite this fragmentation, now enjoys a normalized orthography, a common lexicon, and a normativized grammar for the first time. Although this did not necessarily ensure its survival, it did set standard Basque on the right path.

Publishing those resolutions in the Language Section of the Secretariat of Baiona inspired all the *euskaltzales* (roughly translated as Basque language and culture enthusiasts) to start following these resolutions and specifically called on Euskaltzaindia, the Royal Academy of the Basque Language, to analyze and approve them. Euskaltzaindia responded immediately.

VISIONARY STATESMEN AND A DECLARATION OF PRINCIPLES

Euskaltzaindia decided to address the unification of Basque at the Arantzazu Congress (*Arantzazuko Biltzarrak*) October 3-5, 1968, on the academy's fiftieth anniversary. Standing out among the presenters was Koldo Mitxelena, whose solid linguistic formation and indisputable authority suggested an optimistic beginning to the project. Mitxelena was also the president of the technical commission Euskaltzaindia entrusted with the task of unification. Manuel Lekuona, the chair of Euskaltzaindia at the time, gave a talk titled Orthography. Although it was not limited to orthographic matters, some of which had already been discussed at the Baiona Congress, his talk also analyzed the old lexicon, newly coined words, morphology, and syntax. We do not know with certainty if the president of the technical commission also oversaw the rest of the talks at Arantzazu given by Salbador Garmendia (*Deklinazio* "Declension"), Ambrosi Zatarain (*Euskerazko itz berriak* "New Words of Basque"), and Luis Villasante (*Antzinako euskal hitzen formaz* "On the Form of Old Basque Words"). The only talk with Mitxelena's signature is the one discussed next. Despite the lack of his signature, we surmise that Mitxelena somehow endorsed each of these talks, as he chaired that technical commission.

Before delving into a few linguistic matters, I would like to discuss other more general aspects of the presentation offered at the talk's beginning, precisely because Mitxelena gave a declaration of principles: *Oinharriak. Ze batasunen bila gabiltzan* (Principles. The Unification We Pursue).

This declaration contains nine principles, but we only focus on four here to better understand the spirit of the proposal. The first principle states: *We believe it is indispensable, a matter of life or death, to set Basque on track for unification.* It could be said louder but not clearer. According to the presenter, for Basque to survive, it was imperative to teach the youth the language, and for Basque to be teachable, it inevitably required the unification of the language, especially the unification of the written language. The children enrolled in *ikastolas* during the dictatorship period needed a unified language in which to write and read, even though our *ikastola*, just like any *ikastola*, had a strong dialectal flavor during that time (ours had a markedly western flavor). In those years when everything needed to be created, the need for a normativized and normalized language in the various social spheres was paramount. Teaching ended up also being the driving force of language transmission and diffusion, and history proved this.

The third principle points out the inevitable: *if we ever unify, our language will lose more than mere trifles: Basque will lose the great variation that is so pleasing to our eyes and ears.* Those fascinated by variation, like me, can only confirm the professor's words. Indeed, the establishment of standard Basque has negative consequences for variation, which is by default constraining and even entails the irreversible loss of many traditional dialects. Basque could not be an exception in this case either: standard Basque evidently and undeniably constrains variation (in any case, many dialects have already disappeared, and many others will disappear soon with or without standard Basque). However, there was only one solution to the dilemma: *we prefer Basque alive more than we dislike its artificial elements* [that emerged as a result of the unification process]. Just like him, we would have also been willing to pay the same price.

The fourth principle anticipates problems when stating that *there is no advancement toward unification without hurting anyone,* and this reflects upon the academy's difficult duties in leadership and guidance, as some forms must be selected over others. Next, this principle established the objectives that the academy aims to accomplish through its resolutions: a) *that the dialects do not separate and grow even more apart from each other*, and b) *that those dialects are brought together to the greatest extent possible.*

One last principle, the sixth principle, is worth mentioning because Mitxelena makes a great dialectal proposition that would continue to move ahead: *Nonetheless, it seems that for the needs of written Basque, central dialects are better suited than those on either end, since Basque is seldom heard in Bilbao. Either way, we will all be obliged to compromise, some more than others, if we want to succeed.* He was indeed prescient.

The unification of Basque was a bold proposition but also solid, firm, and well-founded. Standardization was made possible thanks to scientific coherence, historical and social compromise, and the talented vision of statesmen such as Koldo Mitxelena. To them and to all those who followed in their footsteps, our history owes eternal gratitude.

MAKING DECISIONS

Some of the hardest decisions to make were related to conjugated verb forms, which we will come back to, while others concerned nominal inflection, or the forms that nouns take when they bear case or are marked by prepositions. These aspects were published in the proceedings of the Arantzazu Congress titled *Declension*, a term which is still very much used in traditional Basque grammar work. It does not make much sense to discuss how inadequate this term is now. I will avoid using this term when referring to case, postpositions, or other inflectional nominal morphemes, but its use does not distort the proposal's nature. Quite honestly, in the eyes of those who certainly knew how the future of Basque would play out, the discussion about whether to maintain a term such as declension for Basque seemed too trivial.

Case has been discussed in chapter 5, but some of the following aspects are not concerned so much with case marking itself, but the morphological form that words take when bearing case marking. The starting point is the simplest case, the absolutive case, which is the simplest precisely because it has no morphological marking and, in principle, does not create dialectal differences or disagreements with standard Basque. Let's take a noun such as *emakume* "woman" for an example.

A nearly irrefutable truth about Basque dialect grammar is that any noun needs a determiner such as the article *a*. Therefore, in a sentence with an intransitive verb such as *esnatu* "to wake up," the noun *emakume* "woman" requires the article *a* or some other determiner. Since the subjects of intransitive verbs are marked with the absolutive case and this case does not have a visible morphological mark, readers just need to add the article *a* to the noun *emakume* to build at least half of a grammatical sentence.

(94)   Emakume**a** esnatu da
        woman.a.ABS awakened has
        "The woman has awakened"

Remember from chapter 2 that *emakumea* can be translated in English either as "the woman" or as "a woman."

Imagine that the subject of the sentence is not *a* woman, but rather, *the women* or *some women*. In other words, imagine that the subject is now plural (indicated in the example with the gloss PL). In this case, the mark *k* is added, which corresponds to plural marking (and not to the ergative case as the most experienced readers might have guessed). Therefore, we obtain:

(95)   Emakume**ak** esnatu dira
        woman.a.PL.ABS woken up have
        "The women have woken up"

The mechanism does not seem to be too difficult to understand (learning how to use it is a different story). Take a noun and add the article *a*. If the noun is singular, do not add anything else (the singular is the default or unmarked number in world languages, and this is also true in Basque). However, if the noun is plural, add a *k*. English speakers are very familiar with indefinite nouns (i.e., *women* vs. *the women*). The indefinite form in Basque grammar is known as *mugagabea* (meaning unlimited). This indefinite form can appear with certain quantifiers, such as *zenbait* "some" or *hainbat* "many," which are also considered determiners like *a*.

(96) Zenbait emakume esnatu dira
      some woman.ABS woken up have
      "Some women have woken up"

The indefinite form is only a bare noun (*emakume* "woman")—that is, as a word would appear in a dictionary—but this is so only with absolutive marking.

This distinction between definite (singular and plural), and indefinite is also found in all Basque dialects: every single dialect has definite singular, definite plural, and indefinite forms. However, the distinction between plural and indefinite forms has somehow been blurred in certain dialects.

The absolutive case is not particularly problematic, because different dialects share the same forms. However, things get a little more complicated with the ergative case. For instance, the forms that *emakume* "woman" takes in the ergative case for the singular, plural, and indefinite in standard Basque are the following:

(97) a. Emakume**ak** eleberria irakurri du
         woman.a.ERG novel.ABS read has
         "The woman has read the novel"

      b. Emakume**ek** eleberria irakurri dute
         woman.PL.ERG novel.ABS read have
         "The women have read the novel"

      c. Zenbait emakume**k** eleberria irakurri dute
         some woman.ERG novel.ABS read have
         "Some women have read the novel"

In the three forms, the subject is marked with the ergative *k*. That mark is added to the determiner *a* in the singular form *emakumea* "(the) woman"; it is added to the plural morpheme *e* in the plural form *emakumeek* "the women"; and it is added to the bare noun *emakume* in (*zenbait*) *emakumek* "some women." These forms are found in Eastern dialects, but in many western and central varieties, there is only one single form *emakumeak* for both singular and plural—although such a distinction is marked through accentuation, with an accentually marked plural form. Thus, the unification of Basque occurred successfully by considering what apparently seemed like trivial decisions, such as whether the plural form of the ergative case should be *emakumeak* or *emakumeek*, without offending dialectal sensitivities, even though doing so was an almost impossible task. However, it is the case that when we add more and more apparently trivial decisions, the final decision becomes an inevitably much deeper and more controversial matter. This is what happened during the normativization of Basque.

For instance, when looking at dative forms, the puzzle is again very similar to the one previously described. As readers already know, the marking for the dative case is *i*. Regardless of case, a determiner is always added to the noun, such as the article *a* for singular forms or the morpheme *e* for plural forms. In singular forms, there is an intruder that takes the form of *r* and corresponds to the historic demonstrative **har*, from which the article *a* derives (currently the demonstratives are: *hau* "this," *hori* "that," *hura* "that over there"). On the other hand, indefinite forms contain another *r*, analogous in this case: an epenthetic consonant *r* that distinguishes the nominal root vowel (*e*) from the case-marking vowel (*i*). This is at least how José Ignacio Hualde makes this distinction. Hualde is a phonologist and linguist born in central Spain and raised in Madrid, whose father was originally from northeastern Navarre (Uztárroz to be precise), and who learned Basque in the *Euskal Etxea* (roughly translated as Basque Center) in Madrid. Today, he is a world-renowned expert of not only Basque but also synchronic and diachronic phonology of Spanish, as well as Romance languages more generally. These are the three forms:

(98) a. Emakume**ari**
      woman.to.DAT
      "To the woman"

     b. Emakume**ei**
      woman. PL.DAT
      "To (the) women"

     c. Zenbait emakume**ri**
      some woman.r.DAT
      "To some women"

In northeastern dialects, the dative plural form is not *i* as in standard Basque, but rather *er*. Thus, the northeastern form was not the chosen one in this case.

These important decisions were also dialectally biased. Other decisions, however, turned out to be even more morphologically traumatic. These instances aside, let's focus on postpositions, which have not been thoroughly studied either in Basque grammar or generally in grammar and have still been somehow neglected in this book up to this point. As mentioned in chapter 3, postpositions are like prepositions; in fact, they belong to the same category. However, postpositions do not precede their complements (in which case these would be prepositions instead of postpositions), but instead postpositions follow their complements, as their name indicates. In other words, a postposition is the mirror image of a preposition. Two examples are *kin* and *tzat*, which are the mirror images of the English prepositions *with* and *for*, respectively. Both postpositions, *kin* ("with") and *tzat* ("for"), are added to a base that already contains the genitive. The following are examples of genitives:

(99) a. Emakume**aren** eskua
        woman.a.GEN hand.a.ABS
        "The woman's hand"

      b. Emakume**en** eskuak
        woman.PL.GEN hand.PL.ABS
        "The women's hands"

      c. Zenbait emakume**ren** eskuak
        some woman.GEN hand.PL.ABS
        "Some women's hands"

Therefore, if we want to say "for the woman," we start with
the form *emakumearen* (which contains the noun *emakume*, the
article *a(r)*, and the genitive *en*) to which the postposition *tzat*
("for") is added, resulting thus in *emakumearentzat*. That's it!
By contrast, if we want to say "for the women," we start with
the genitive plural form *emakumeen* and add *tzat* to build a
complex Lego block like *emakumeentzat*. That's right! And to
finish things off, "for some women" would of course be *zenbait emakumerentzat*, always remembering the phonological
intruder *r*.

Similarly, the postposition *kin* ("with") is added to the genitive form, but in this case, the latter loses the final *n*, generating
the following grammatical forms:

(100) a. Emakumea**rekin**
          woman.a.GEN.with
          "With the woman"

        b. Emakume**ekin**
          woman.PL.GEN.with
          "With the women"

        c. Zenbait emakume**rekin**
          some woman.GEN.with
          "With some women"

In the postposition *kin* "with," the final *n* of the genitive *(r)* *en* disappears, and this makes **emakumearenkin*, etc. ungrammatical. These forms with *kin*, known as the *sociative* or *comitative* case in Basque grammar, have the variants *ki* and *kila*, which suggests a more sophisticated analysis while *kin*, *kila* would break down as *ki* plus *n* or *ki* plus *la*. In fact, the locative postposition *n* is similar to the English preposition *in*. We will not continue breaking morphemes down because we do not want our readers to throw in the towel. Besides, this is a field of grammar that is under construction, so wear a helmet! Therefore, to express "with the woman," speakers have to choose among *emakumearekin*, *emakumeareki*, and *emakumearekila*, as well as another considerably different form found in western dialects: *emakumeagaz*. The difference between *emakumearekin* (standard Basque) and *emakumeagaz* (western dialect) is considerable: the first form has the genitive as its base, while the second form contains the morphemes *ga* and *z*. The morpheme *ga* appears with other locative postpositions in animate nouns, such as *emakumearengan* "in the woman" or *emakumearengana* "to the woman." The morpheme *z*, on the other hand, is the same morpheme attributed to the *instrumental* postpositions (*aizkoraz* "with the ax"), as mentioned in Mitxelena's presentation. As a matter of fact, it might be the case that the *z* mark shared by *emakumeagaz* "with the woman" (attributed to the sociative or comitative postposition) and *aizkoraz* "with the ax" (attributed to the instrumental postposition) is the same *z* postposition, which may or may not be accompanied by other morphemes.

Now that standard Basque has already been created and consolidated, we can devote ourselves to other more peripheral theoretical discussions. Half a century ago though, the key issue was this: there was plenty to choose from, and they were forced to make choices. Choosing one form over another did not mean that the others were not as legitimate—for instance, in his presentation, Mitxelena discussed the form *gaz* and its legitimacy in Biscayan as an alternative to *kin* in other dialectal regions.

Making choices is not easy, and they were bold enough to do so. Time applauds their bravery.

LONG-TERM MEMORY

If nominal inflection was rich, verbal inflection had (and still has) an overwhelming number of possibilities for morphological variation for any speaker, Basque or not. We have already carefully discussed verbal forms, but it is worth briefly mentioning some of their aspects here.

A delicate matter regarding verbs that also required consensus was the question of Basque verbal roots. This was especially true of the subjunctive and imperative modes when compared to the indicative mode, which we already analyzed in chapter 4 without mentioning it by name.

As mentioned in the beginning of this chapter, Basque grammar alternates between "to be" and "to have" for indicative forms. Regarding the subjunctive and imperative modes, however, two different verbal roots are found in Basque dialects: *di* for intransitive forms and *za* for transitive forms. In terms of grammar, there are two auxiliaries **edin* and **ezan*, which are only used in conjugated forms but not in participle or other nonconjugated forms (since they are historically reconstructed forms, they are preceded by an asterisk). I will adopt a cautious attitude in discussing these roots without digressing to explain what they truly conceal. These verbal roots appear in their conjugated forms in different types of subordinate clauses, for example:

(101) a. Argia piztu dut umea lasai da**din**
        light turned on have kid calm down AUX
        "I have turned on the light, so that the kid calms down"

       b. Argia piztu dut umeak esnea har de**zan**
        light turned on have kid milk drink AUX
        "I have turned on the light, so that the kid drinks milk"

All these subjunctive forms have a final *n* morpheme.

Furthermore, these forms have a peculiarity that has not yet been mentioned: the participle for the verbs "to calm down" and "to get" are *lasaitu* and *hartu*, respectively. However, the forms in the examples listed above are *lasai* and *har*, both without the participle morpheme *tu*. These nonconjugated verb forms without *tu* are known as *verb bases* in Basque grammar, and in standard Basque, they are clearly different from participle forms. One of the contexts where these verb bases are found is precisely in the above exemplified subjunctive forms—which are translated into present-tense indicative forms in English. Compared to these standard forms (as well as to those of central and eastern varieties) nonetheless, western forms have two very important differences. The first difference is that in these verbs, western forms maintain the perfective participle with *tu*, as opposed to the verb base of standard Basque. The second difference is that western forms do not have the root *za*, but rather *gi* in conjugated transitive verb forms.

(102) a. Argia piztu dot umea lasaitu daiten
        light turned on have kid calm down AUX
        "I have turned on the light, so that the kid calms down"

       b. Argia piztu dot umeak esnea hartu da**gi**an
        light turned on have kid milk drink AUX
        "I have turned on the light, so that the kid gets milk"

Put simply, in the subjunctive form, we have *lasai dadin* (standard) vs. *lasaitu daiten* (western) for "to calm down," and *har dezan* (standard) vs. *hartu dagian* (western) for "to get." As discussed before, these were also some of the matters upon which the creators of what is now standard Basque needed to agree. These discussions are documented in the presentation's references (and the proceedings). Even for apparently small details, Mitxelena's presentation is illuminating. Regarding this specific problem, Mitxelena emphasizes the need to distinguish both forms exactly the way they are used in many dialects: on the one hand, the perfective participle *tu* in forms such as *sartu da* "has entered"—in the indicative and with *tu*—and on the other hand, the verb base without *tu* in forms such as *sar bedi* or *sar dadin* "so he/she/it may enter"—in the subjunctive and without *tu*— (even though he does not use the terms perfective participle and verb base so generalized now in Basque grammar). Mitxelena also reminds those with long-term memory problems that this distinction was also found in old Biscayan (and not only this distinction but also the root *za* of standard Basque was found in old Biscayan).

Another wise choice from that proposal was giving priority to those common forms that distanced themselves the least in the majority of dialects, such as the pluralizer *it* as opposed to the morpheme *z* generalized in western forms (liburuak ekarri d*it*u vs. liburuak ekarri dau*z*, both meaning "(s)he has brought the books"). Yet another wise choice was prioritizing the old forms documented in the literature as opposed to more innovative (and localized) forms.

The proposal of the Unified Basque Verb (*Aditz laguntzaile batua*) was published a few years later in 1973. In 1979, the Grammar Commission (*Gramatika Batzordea*) of the Academy was created and has since developed the most complete grammar of the Basque language, available now as *Euskal Gramatika Lehen Urratsak* (Basque Grammar: First Steps), as mentioned in chapter 1.

It contains seven volumes, the first of which was published in 1985 (which, as Pello Salaburu remembers, was typed because it was provisional and under debate) and continued until 2011 when the project was finished. This grammar text is a must-read reference for all those interested in Basque grammar in one way or another. Given that it is an academic grammar proposal, its purpose is to normativize language, particularly written language. In any case, normativizing language goes hand in hand with describing language, which requires consultation and knowledge of literary texts containing different dialects written during different periods, and eventually choosing one over another. The academy's grammar is thus a normative grammar that prescribes certain uses to the detriment of others. Readers are probably more familiar with normative grammars because of their academic experience.

However, time does not go by in vain, and this can also be appreciated in the evolution of these volumes. Not only did the project finalize but so did an era. Luckily, normativization is not an endless task.

When the Grammar Commission began its course, normativization was still very young, and the language lacked the vast literary corpus that it has today. True literary gems were and are being written throughout the last and current centuries, as is being acknowledged both inside and out of the Basque Country. It is true that bad literature is also published and consumed, which reflects the normalization efforts of a community. Basque is not only learned in *ikastolas* and schools, but also in high schools, vocational schools, and universities. If we meddle in our children's academic lives, we will realize that textbooks are often a delight. Science is published in Basque; conferences covering a variety of topics are organized in Basque and seemingly with as much ease as in English. Basque is perfectly equipped to face any difficulties of a formal nature, which was not impossible but was considerably more difficult before the creation of standard Basque. There is a Basque newspaper (*Berria*) and a number of different publications. We forge the path by walking it.

The Grammar Commission of the Academy set new and probably more descriptive and flexible challenges regarding certain aspects of syntactic and morphological variation. To think that the Grammar Commission is and will be devoted to outdated practices of linguists buried in unintelligible theoretical dissertations—as we have heard more than once—is to have absolutely no idea what theoretical grammar is. Theoretical grammar is developed in a scientific environment in which academic work can be found. When our college students take *Hizkuntzalaritza I* (or *Intro to Linguistics*), they learn the difference between theoretical and normative grammar. For instance, Patxi Goenaga and Beñat Oihartzabal are exceptional linguists whose knowledge guides their work in the academy. However, their normative work in the academy is different from their theoretical work. Their scientific contributions are well known and acclaimed outside our own boundaries (although not as highly as our best Basque novels); their contribution to the normativization of Basque is just another sphere where they have developed their work. Let's not confuse the terms.

Right now, Basque has other concerns. On the one hand, its usage by adolescents especially, although not only necessarily, seems to suffer from a transitory linguistic amnesia that pushes them to speak in Spanish among their peers, even though they were all raised speaking Basque. Why would I lie to my readers who have patiently accompanied me throughout this journey? Yes, languages such as Spanish and French have a strong impact and can eradicate a tiny little language such as ours in one generation. The future of our most disadvantaged minority languages is only guaranteed through preservation. I hope readers do not feel tempted to suggest that Spanish and French are endangered languages in Basque territory. Of course, readers can always disagree, but they cannot deceive themselves. On the other hand, another concern for Basque paradoxically has to do with the flip side of standard Basque, that is, with usage in nonformal registers. Nonformal registers are found in local varieties and dialects in which Basque speakers express themselves naturally, spontaneously, and with familiarity to talk about mundane issues, whereas standard Basque is used in more linguistically formal situations, particularly by those speakers of local varieties. As for speakers of areas where Basque ceased to be spoken before its standardization, different forms of unified Basque are emerging. Additionally, unified Basque-dialect mixing is becoming more and more common, particularly on the radio.

Hence, the key is to veer neither starboard nor portside but, rather, to keep traversing the great paths navigated by great sailors—many of them Basque, such as Juan Sebastián Elcano or Andrés Urdaneta—as well as the lesser-known routes if they still exist, and, of course, to sail them in our language.

APPENDIX

Koldo Zuazo's doctoral dissertation on the standardization of Basque is titled *Euskararen batasuna* (*The Unification of Basque*) and was published by Euskaltzaindia in the *Iker* collection volume number 5 in Bilbao in 1988. Zuazo's *Standard Basque and its Dialects* was also published by Routledge in 2019. I strongly encourage reading this book for those readers interested in the historic details of the process, which cannot be fully understood without comprehending the historic evolution of Basque and the historical, political, and social circumstances that Basque has experienced for centuries.

I also recommend Pello Salaburu's article "El euskera contemporáneo: el largo camino de la unificación literaria" published in *Historia de la lengua vasca* and edited by Joaquín Gorrotxategi, Ivan Igartua, and Joseba A. Lakarra in 2018 (Vitoria-Gasteiz, Basque Govern). The article analyzes the decades from the 1960s to the present using objective data from a more personal perspective, which makes the reading appealing and fun. *The Agreements of the Baiona Congress* (Baiona'ko Biltzarraren Erabakiak) that were referenced here were published in the popular journal *Jakin*, volume number 18, pages 20–28, in 1965. It can be accessed through the journal's website.

The decisions made with regard to the unification of Basque at the 1968 *Arantzazu Congress* organized by Euskaltzindia, as well as Koldo Mitxelena's presentation, are published in the journal *Euskera 13* (1968) under the title of *Arantzazuko Biltzarrak 1968 urriaren 3, 4 eta 5ean* (Arantzazu Congress June 3, 4, and 5, 1968) and is available entirely online. Mitxelena's presentation can be found on pages 203–219. The declaration of principles can also be found on pages 203–204. The translation of the text is ours.

Those interested in a detailed analysis of the forms that nouns take when bearing case and postpositions should consult José Ignacio Hualde's chapter "Case and number inflection of noun phrases," published in *A Grammar of Basque* (2003), previously cited in chapter 1 and edited by Dr. Hualde himself and Jon

Ortiz de Urbina, referencing pages 171–194. I thank Dr. Hualde for the specifics regarding the analogical *r* in the forms *zenbait emakumeri* "to some women," etc.

Even though it is a technical text that requires considerable theoretical knowledge, I also want to cite Ane Berro's outstanding doctoral dissertation *Breaking verbs: from event structure to syntactic categories in Basque*, which earned the author a joint doctoral degree at the University of the Basque Country (UPV/ EHU) and the Université Bordeaux Montaigne. It is an excellent read for any initiated linguist. In her thesis, she explores the lexical and syntactic status of the suffix *tu* and the light verb *egin* "to do" in the formation of Basque predicates.

The reference to the usage of the perfective participle (with *tu*) and the verb base (without *tu*) were extracted from Mitxelena's presentation at the Arantzazu Congress, already cited. The text, as well as the translation we provided, can be found at the beginning of page 218. The original version explains:

Hori da, hain zuzen, batasunerako bidea, neure iritziz, baina, batasunera nahi ez dutenek ere ikas bezate, bederen noiz kendu behar diren tu eta *i* horiek eta noiz utzi dauden daudenean. Nahasmendura goaz bestela, ez batasunera.

[This is precisely, in my opinion, the path toward unification. But those who do not want this unification should still learn when to drop and when to keep -*tu* and -*i*. If not, this is chaos and we won't go toward any sort of unification.]

I will omit the original texts about the principles extracted from the talk, cited and commented upon in the text.

The proposal *Aditz laguntzaile batua*, which analyzes the unified auxiliary verb, was published in 1973 in the Academy's journal *Euskera 18*, and it is preceded by some of Koldo Mitxelena's explanations and clarification as signed on August 10, 1973.

7

Variety is the Spice of Life

Variety is the spice of life. Basque and Michelin stars. Standard, prestige, and dialectal distance. Born under an unlucky star. Cuisine with and without complexes: mischievous and sneaky chefs. Culinary déjà vu. Pintxo bar. There's no place like home.

VARIETY IS THE SPICE OF LIFE

Unified Basque, or standard Basque, was a great achievement for the history, dissemination, and eventual consolidation of the Basque language. Now that this middle aged unified Basque is in very good shape and enjoys prestige as well as extraordinary literary accolades, we should discuss the flip side of the coin, that is, linguistic variation.

First, however, I want to make a declaration of principles. I would like to make it very clear that having reflected on variation and even having devoted a great part of my research to analyzing and finding an explanation for variation, I cannot help but state the obvious: despite the (relatively important) differences attested in different varieties, all Basque speakers share the same language, and therefore, they also share many linguistic aspects that should neither be ignored nor underrated. Now that I have established that there is a common language bigger than the varieties, it is only fair to mention that the standardization of Basque allowed us to create a variety appropriate to our time, serving as a versatile tool for education, administration, media, scientific writing, translation, and literature, among other fields.

It has provided us with a vehicle to disseminate Basque through a common variety that facilitates exchange among speakers from distant varieties that might otherwise be nearly unintelligible. Unified Basque changed our lives and keeps us going. But beyond this unified variety and beyond this common language, a number of varieties have been documented that differ from each other in many ways. These varieties create a world of rich scents and flavors that make life for any Basque speaker—who is used to great culinary pleasures—an incomparable sensory experience. Variety is indeed the spice of life.

BASQUE AND MICHELIN STARS

Regarding taste, nothing is written in stone, even though certain tastes are much better appreciated and more highly praised than others. Basque cuisine is a fierce type of cuisine that amazes and satisfies visitors' palates as well as our own. This is why Basque cuisine boasts a whole Michelin sky full of stars scattered around forty restaurants throughout the Basque Country. This culinary success turned our country into a divine destination for foodies from around the world, regardless of their origin or condition.

The Michelin Guide ranking system awards from one up to three Michelin stars. Three stars indicate "exceptional cuisine that is worth a special journey," two stars denote "excellent cooking that is worth a detour," and one star means "a very good restaurant in its category." One, two, and three-star restaurants are scattered throughout (almost) every Basque region. Out of the seven provinces that form the Basque Country, all of them except for Zuberoa (Soule), the easternmost province, has at least one Michelin-starred restaurant. If we take a closer look at the map though, stars are clustered in certain geographic regions, especially in Donostia, Bilbao, and Biarritz-Angelu-Baiona (known as BAB). Without the intention of undervaluing the one- and two-star restaurants, the Basque restaurants that received the illustrious three-star rating in 2016 need no introduction: Arzak, owned by Juan Mari Arzak, and Akelarre, owned by Pedro Subijana, both in Donostia; Martin Berasategui, owned by Martin Berasategui, in Lasarte-Oria, also in Gipuzkoa; and Azurmendi, owned by Eneko Atxa in Larrabetzu, Bizkaia, also notable for having one of our youngest chefs at the helm. In 2019, these four restaurants all maintained their three-star ratings, and thirty-three other Basque restaurants spread throughout six Basque provinces were also awarded one and two Michelin stars. It is worth mentioning that the Basque Country has the highest number of Michelin star restaurants per square-mile in the world.

Basques are proud people, so naturally we take pride in our greatest chefs. But we are even more proud to know that these four chefs also speak Basque, and this allows not only our cuisine but also our vehicular language to traverse difficult frontiers.

These top-notch chefs all share a deep love for cuisine and language, but they all have their quirks both in and out of their kitchens. Despite our fondness for cuisine, which does not make us experts, let's turn our attention to linguistic matters, which we certainly can handle with expertise. All these chefs are Basque speakers. While Arzak, Subijana, and Berasategui speak the central dialect, Atxa speaks the western dialect (and his restaurant is in the westernmost area of the region—something like the Wild West, according to those central dialect speakers who suffer from a certain dialectocentric syndrome). Andoni Luis Aduriz, owner of the two Michelin-starred restaurants in Mugaritz, Errenteria, is also a Basque speaker—and for the record, Mugaritz was declared as the seventh-best restaurant in the British magazine Restaurant's annual list of "The World's 50 Best Restaurants" in 2016 and 2019. We can proudly say that Atxondo—whose chef, Bittor Arginzoniz, is also a Basque speaker—was awarded the title of third-best restaurant by the same magazine in 2019. Many other one-starred restaurants are on the coast in Getari, in Bidarte (Bidart), or in Biarritz, where the kostatarra dialect is spoken ("coastal" dialect as named by Koldo Zuazo, whose dialectal geographic vision of Basque we follow in this text). From the coast eastward, a few other starred restaurants are scattered, for instance in Senpere (Saint-Pée-Sur-Nivelle) and Ainhoa, as well as in Firmin Arrambide's Les Pyrénées in the capital of Lower Navarre, where Navarro-Lapurdian is spoken.

Adventurous foodies who want a unique culinary experience have plenty from which to choose, and if they want to season the experience with certain dialectal flavors, they can go west to east or east to west, passing through the central region and stopping there to explore not only the essence of our food but the great secrets of its diversity.

STANDARD, PRESTIGE, AND DIALECTAL DISTANCE

We do not really know why Donostia—or Donostialdea, if you prefer—and its surroundings shine so brightly with all their Michelin stars. There are probably generational and histori-cal reasons to explain the phenomenon. Experts talk about *el grupo de los doce* ("the gang of twelve"), among whom Arzak and Subijana can be found, as well as some other popular chefs. For instance, Karlos Arguiñano has enjoyed high ratings on national television for years, and Luis Irizar, the master of masters, earned the first Michelin star in the sky of Basque cuisine.

The gang of twelve essentially created and, years later, showed the world what is today known as the New Basque Cuisine, which allowed for younger chefs, such as Atxa or Aduriz, to be trained in a very particular way of understanding cuisine. All of them have brought Basque gastronomy to the top of interna-tional cuisine.

They established our cuisine's standards, which are now asso-ciated with indisputable and well-deserved prestige. They rein-vented traditional Basque cuisine, passed on for generations.

Differences between gastronomy and linguistics aside, the reinvention of standard Basque by great chefs toiling over lin-guistic stoves allowed for the renewal, preservation, and dissem-ination of our ancestral language not only in our country but worldwide. This task was even more challenging considering that standard Basque was not merely built upon the characteristics of central dialects—even if standard Basque, just like Basque cuisine, is deeply rooted in and closest to central ingredients—but also allows speakers of central dialects to safely, comfortably, and joyously use the standard. This safety and this certainty, nonetheless, become perhaps more vulnerable as the gap between the spoken dialect and standard Basque widens.

For the record, feeling more vulnerable as the dialectal distance from the standard increases is not an exception for Basque. These issues that plague Basque speakers are the same issues that might afflict speakers of any other language. The perception of the (supposed) strengths and weaknesses of our dialect is subjectively measured on the basis of its distance, explicit or not, from the standard variety.

BORN UNDER AN UNLUCKY STAR

Under the bright starry sky, so full of stars that dim and die as well as those that never light up at all, there is light and darkness, and there are also lucky and unlucky—good and bad—chefs and restaurants. Being the polite people we are, we do not make assumptions, since many of them manage to survive and earn a decent salary. I am sure that bad chefs are absolutely exceptional, which makes me reaffirm the rule: Basque cuisine is extraordinary and has excellent chefs, regardless of the star under which they were born.

We Basques are pretty lavish regarding culinary matters but sometimes even more so when it comes to linguistic matters, especially unfortunate linguistic phenomena: maybe not entirely unfortunate, but at least these are phenomena that do not align with many Basque speakers' intuitions, or standard Basque. Let's discuss some examples.

In certain Basque varieties, the object of a transitive sentence is marked differently from the canonical marking that is found in most other dialects and in standard Basque. We have already discussed canonical object marking, so readers should not find the next example too difficult to understand.

(103) Enarak Jon ikusi du
       Enara.ERG Jon.ABS seen has
       "Enara has seen Jon"

In this transitive sentence, the subject (Enara, a girl's name meaning "swallow") is marked with the ergative *k* (like Sherlock in chapter 5), and the object (Jon) is marked with the absolutive case (like Watson also in chapter 5). Readers might remember that the absolutive case is the morphologically unmarked or default case (that is why Jon is simply Jon, without any case marker).

By contrast, in certain varieties, this object is not marked with the absolutive case, but rather with a different case, the dative, as shown in the example below:

(104) Enarak Joni ikusi dio
       Enara.ERG Jon.DAT seen to-him-has
       "Enara has seen Jon"

Indeed, Jon (object of the sentence) carries the morphological marker *i*, which corresponds to the dative case in Basque.

The dative marker in (104) is not the canonical marker of the direct object and does not follow the rules explicitly prescribed by Euskaltzaindia, the Royal Academy of the Basque Language. This marker would be canonical in a sentence such as the following when Jon is the indirect object:

(105) Enarak Joni eskua eman dio
       Enara.ERG Jon.DAT hand.ABS given tohimithas
       "Enara has given Jon her hand"

However, the marker *i* for Jon in the transitive sentence (104) does not follow the rules of either standard Basque or many other varieties. For most speakers, this sentence in (104) is ungrammatical and, therefore, deserves not a Michelin star, but only the asterisk that grammarians use to indicate ill-formed sentences. Most speakers perceive this dative marker as a substitute for the canonical absolutive marker, like seasoning meat with sugar instead of pepper and salt or sprinkling French toast with salt instead of cinnamon and powdered sugar.

Furthermore, this matter not only concerns heterodox direct object marking, but it also extends to verbal inflection. Instead of using the canonical bipersonal form *du*, the tripersonal form *dio* includes a dative agreement marker *o* that is assigned to Jon. In other words, the dative agreement marker replaces the absolutive one. Dative marking resembles Spanish *leísmo*, that is, the substitution of the dative agreement marker for the accusative one. Both examples are again illustrated below, the one cooked according to the canon's recipe (a) and the other violating it (b).

(106) a. Enarak Jon ikusi du
        Enara.ERG Jon.ABS seen him-has

     b. Enarak Joni ikusi dio
        Enara.ERG Jon.DAT seen to-him-has

This noncanonical way of cooking casual object markers is not merely attested with objects like Jon. You and I, for instance, can also be cooked, breaking the canon in these varieties. Example (107b) can be compared with an alternate canonical example (107a) as follows:

(107) a. Enarak ni ikusi nau
        Enara.ERG I.ABS seen me-has
        "Enara has seen me"

     b. Enarak niri ikusi dit
        Enara.ERG I.DAT seen to-me-has
        "Enara has seen me"

The issue with first- and second- (whether singular or plural) person objects is even more drastic for two main reasons concerning the object marker and verbal inflection. Firstly, the object *ni* "I" takes the dative marker *i* instead of the absolutive marker. Secondly, because the object is assigned the dative agreement marker *t* of the form *dit* instead of the canonical absolutive agreement marker *na* of the form *nau*, the tripersonal form (*dit*) replaces the bipersonal form (*nau*). The concern is that in this heterodox cuisine—where the non-canonical tripersonal form *dit* replaces the canonical bipersonal form *nau*—the genuine canonical form has disappeared in many cases. Thus, in these varieties, if the agreement marker doubling were to be omitted, apparently one single verb form would appear with both a transitive verb (108a) and a ditransitive verb (108b).

(108) a. ikusi dit
          seen to-me-has
          "(S)he has seen me"

       b. eman dit
          given to-me-it-has
          "(S)he has given it to me"

Now readers might rightfully ask themselves who dare mix condiments in such an extravagant way, but they might be surprised to find out that Basque cuisine is naturally over-the-top (if these features can be considered as such, which we honestly doubt). Koldo Zuazo, the extraordinary dialectology expert of our particular linguistic gastronomy, says that this is basically how all Navarrese Basque is cooked. These unique flavors can be tasted in the Ulzama valley (in the central region), in Esteribar and the Erro (Erroibar) valley (in the east), and in transitional varieties of Aezkoa and Baztan.

Western Basque is also part of this heterodox cuisine, which is attested in Basauri, Igorre, Dima (westernmost region), Forua and Gernika (in Busturialdea), Lekeitio (in the east), and Elgoibar (transitional variety). Even central varieties recognize this flavor, such as those spoken in Tolosa, Ordizia and Goierri, Lasarte-Oria (where the three Michelin-starred restaurant Berasategui is located), Pasaia, Oiartzun, Hondarribia, Irun, Imotz, Basaburua Mayor, and Larraun. Moreover, informal standard Basque is also part of this extravagant way of cooking.

But one can find eccentric cuisines like this one outside Basque boundaries. What is most captivating is that a linguaphile can find very similar eccentricities in the menus of other languages around the world. Linguistic typologists have long had evidence of this phenomenon called *differential object marking*. We Basques are neither exceptional nor different in our dialectal eccentricities.

CUISINE WITH AND WITHOUT COMPLEXES: MISCHIEVOUS AND SNEAKY CHEFS
More could be said about the eccentric and extravagant nature of differential object marking; we must tolerate eccentricity and extravagance to some extent, but the data presented here are probably some of the most stigmatized and discredited data gathered among the multiple and varied phenomena attested to in Basque varieties.

Perhaps the problem is that speakers who do not use this marking system condemn it, but this prejudice also penetrates the consciences of those speakers whose varieties allow this feature. Therefore, when linguists attentively address this problem without prejudice, they come across sneaky chefs who repeatedly confess that they simply do not speak properly, so linguists should study other speakers from different varieties where the "correct," and therefore, deserving of scientific attention, forms are used. For this reason, it is necessary to explain to these speakers that linguists are really interested in whichever forms speakers use. In other words, linguistic interest does not focus on what is considered refined, world-renowned canonical cuisine, but on humble local fare.

There are, however, some other mischievous chefs who are perfectly aware of the canon and still defend their own usage, which both relieves and satisfies curious linguists, because we can finally sink our teeth into their local delicacies. Below is an extract of a conversation between the dialectologist Aitor Iglesias and a speaker from Dima—a variety that allows for differential object marking:

"How do you say *I've seen you?*" asks the dialectologist.

"*Ikusi dotzut,*" the speaker produces the form attested in their variety.

"And *ikusi saitut?*" the dialectologist mentions the canonical form to the speaker.

"No, no, no, I know I should be saying *ikusi saitut,* but I say *ikusi dotzut.*"

"And you never use it?" says the dialectologist, referring to the canonical form.

"No, never. That Basque is not . . . our Basque. It's wrong, but whatever; good or bad, it's ours."

The last answer from the dialect speaker shows *covert prestige.* They opt for their local variety even though their Basque is, in their own words, *wrong.* The preference for the local variety shows that sometimes speakers favor group identity (covert prestige) over overt prestige associated to standard Basque.

A suspicious kitchen is no longer suspect once we get close enough to carefully see, smell, and taste the food. In that moment, you realize that it has nothing to do with improperly seasoning the meat with sugar. There is nothing eccentric, but rather a type of unconventional cuisine that does obey other well-known linguistic norms like Michael Silverstein's *animacy hierarchy,* which seems to govern many grammatical aspects crosslinguistically. At the top of this hierarchy, there are first-person pronouns (I), followed by second-person pronouns (you), and then third-person pronouns (he/she). As we go down the hierarchy's rungs, we find person names (Jon) first, followed by human animate nouns (woman), then nonhuman animate nouns (quail or sea bass), and finally inanimate nouns (television) at the bottom. In this apparently random cuisine, nonetheless, differential object marking does not mark every object (with the dative case) but, only marks the objects ranked highest in the animacy hierarchy. Therefore, no Basque dialect that manifests this phenomenon allows for *quails, sea bass,* or *televisions* to be marked with the dative case.

This finding shows that object marking is restricted by principles that are inherent to languages or varieties. Furthermore, these are very strong restrictions as shown by the following ungrammatical example in (a), which has only one possible grammatical alternative: the canonical alternative in (b) that marks the object with the absolutive case.

(109) a. *Enarak telebistari ikusi dio
           Enara.ERG television.DAT seen to-it-has
           "Enara has watched television"

       b. Enarak telebista ikusi du
          Enara.ERG television.ABS seen has

Languages or their varieties somehow choose where to segment the hierarchy. For example, certain varieties allow for marking the object with the dative case only when it is in the first or second person, and this object marking is obligatory. In Lekeitio, in which differential object marking is also optional, the phenomenon occurs with second-person, third person, person names, and human animate nouns (as long as they refer unquestionably to humans and not nonhuman animals or objects).

CULINARY DÉJÀ VU

At this point in the chapter, the most refined foodies among our readers have probably already experienced the feeling of having visited the Basque Country and tasted Basque cuisine, even if they have not yet actually done either. It is presumably a true culinary déjà vu that takes our readers from dialectal Basque cuisine to that of their own kitchens, that is, English. Moreover, it might not even be the English kitchen it takes them to, which we will discuss soon, but perhaps to the most canonical, widespread dishes.

Below is our example of a transitive sentence, which we will now analyze in English:

(110) Enara has seen Jon

In Basque, the direct object can be marked canonically or noncanonically with the absolutive or dative case respectively. In English, on the other hand, there are no overt object markers. English has almost completely lost its case system with the exception of personal pronouns, which can take the nominative case (i.e., *I, he/she, they*), the accusative case (i.e., *me, him/her, them*), or the possessive case (i.e., *mine, his/hers, their*). In the example below, the personal pronoun *him* bears the accusative case.

(111)   Enara has seen him

What is marked by case in Basque is often marked either with a preposition or with very restrictive word order in English. Readers might remember the previously discussed instrumental (INS), comitative (COM), and locative (LOC) cases:

(112)   Jon trenez etorri da
        Jon train.INS come has
        "Jon has come **by** train"

(113)   Jon Lorearekin etorri da
        Jon Lorea.COM come has
        "Jon has come **with** Lorea"

(114)   Jon ikastolan dago
        Jon ikastola.LOC is
        "Jon is **at** the ikastola"

In these examples, in Basque, case is marked by the postpositions *(e)z, (re)kin*, and *n*, whereas in the English versions, it is marked by the prepositions *by, with*, and *at*, respectively. As mentioned before, English also allows for double object constructions in which the dative case is assigned through word order.

(115)   Enara gave a kiss [to Jon.DAT]

(116)   Enara gave [Jon.DAT] a kiss

(117)   *Enara gave a kiss Jon

In example (115), the indirect object *Jon* is a prepositional phrase, introduced by the preposition *to*, that bears the dative case. In example (116), however, there is no preposition, just a bare noun phrase. In double-object constructions, the verb takes two noun phrases, where the dative argument (i.e., the indirect object) always precedes the accusative argument (i.e., the direct object). This word order is absolutely constraining and does not allow for direct objects to precede indirect objects, such as in (117), which in turn, allows English speakers to easily identify the cases of both arguments. In Basque, although the order of the arguments is very flexible, there is only one possible way to say this sentence:

(118)   Enarak musua eman dio Joni

The subject *Enara* is marked with the ergative case (*k*), the direct object *musua* is marked with the absolutive case (∅), and the indirect object *Jon* bears the dative case (*i*). In canonical standard Basque, the dative marking *i* marks indirect objects such as *Jon* in (118). In noncanonical dialectal Basque, however, the dative-bearing postposition (*i*) extends to direct objects, and the auxiliary also contains the dative agreement marker *o*.

(119)   Enarak Joni ikusi dio

However, Basque is very restrictive when selecting the direct objects that can be marked with the dative marker *i*. A Basque variety that allows for noncanonical constructions such as the previous example (119) would not allow for the following construction because inanimate direct objects cannot take the dative case:

(120)   *Enarak telebistari ikusi dio

Thus, even in the most permissive dialectal Basque, speakers say: *Enarak telebista ikusi du*. It could be said that in many Basque varieties, the dative marking *i* is now used to mark a subset of direct objects with very particular features related to animacy and specificity. While this overextension is spreading fairly quickly, Basque

(dialectal and nondialectal) speakers' perception of this phenomenon is still very prejudiced. A comparable phenomenon in English
is double negation (briefly discussed in chapter 1), where multiple
negations are allowed in the sentence. Read the following canonical and noncanonical examples in English:

(121)   I did**n't** see anybody

(122)   I did**n't** see **no**body

The canonical construction in (121) reflects the prescriptive rule
of standard English: each subject-predicate sentence can only contain one negative form, which in this case is *didn't*. The example
in (122) negates both the auxiliary and the pronoun, making this a
dialectal noncanonical construction that also brings strong negative
attitudes, bias, and reluctance in the English-speaking community.
While the roots of African American speech developed in rural
South of the United States, today the African American speech
has become a trans-regional, ethically based variety of English.
Many artists in the music industry use it as it is a stylistically hot
and appealing trend, a process referred to as commodification.
Readers are probably familiar with Marvin Gaye's classic "Ain't No
Mountain High Enough" or the Rolling Stones' legendary "(I Can't
Get No) Satisfaction," which both use double negatives. It is not
exclusively speakers of this vernacular who use this construction but
also speakers of other English varieties. In fact, this construction
was acceptable in sixteenth-century English. For instance, any *bar-
dolatrous* reader might recognize the quote "I never was, nor never
will be" from Shakespeare's *Richard III*, written about 1593. As time
went by, double negation has been relegated to a dialectal form of
variation and has lost its standardized status among English speakers. Despite the historical, dialectal, and even musical usage of this
construction, today double negation still inspires negative attitudes
toward those speakers who employ it.

        Double negation and differential object marking are some-
what common linguistic phenomena. Double negatives are

common standardized constructions observed in languages such as Hungarian, Romance languages, many African languages, and of course, in our beloved Basque. Differential object marking, on the other hand, is attested to in more than three hundred languages throughout the world, but English is not one of them. Different languages mark these direct objects differently. For instance, Romanian and Spanish use morphemes that derive from prepositions to mark these direct objects; Turkish and Hindi use a morphological case; Maori uses suppletive determiners; and Bantu languages use agreement markers or clitics. In all these different languages, the speakers' perceptions of these phenomena vary dramatically, some languages being more permissive than others. In any case, all these world cuisines are similar in that they allow these phenomena in their kitchens, but the perceptions of these cuisines change, most likely because taste, of both food and language, is of a very personal nature.

PINTXO BAR

Basque gastronomy goes a long way, truth be told, so it is very difficult to choose one restaurant or bar over another. Even once the decision is made, who hasn't ever gotten dizzy when going over an endless menu with too many dishes in certain restaurants (and we won't even mention prices)? For more hesitant foodies (and for economical ones) the go-to answer can always be a pintxo bar. These bars contain a wide variety of high-quality, miniature portions of our exquisite cuisine at a fair price. You do not have to necessarily satisfy yourself in one bar either. You can always barhop and let yourself be carried along by temptation. However, choosing a city or town is somewhat more difficult. It depends on your taste. My favorite destination is still Donostia's Old Town, and, if given the choice, Tamboril on Pescadería Street and Ganbara on San Jerónimo Street (yeah, Donostia and the central dialects once again . . .).

Beyond my probably biased taste, this time I have chosen an award-winning option that has won the international "Top

Choice" award for the second consecutive year. It is the Xukela
bar on El Perro Street in Bilbao's Old Town. In Xukela, there
is a little bit of everything (and of course, it's all good): piquillo
peppers with anchovies and caviar; grilled mushrooms with
cockscomb and sugar-coated with crystalline pepper; grilled
champignon mushrooms with smoked cod and apple cream; crab
cream with pepper; grilled zucchini with garlic cheese, salmon,
and fine herbs . . .

I could go on . . .

The morphological and syntactic variety of Basque is like
a long pintxo bar, be it Xukela or any other bar in the Basque
Country that I suggest readers try. Without surpassing the limits
of verbal inflection, our dialectal gastronomy is based on a delicious microvariation. This bar should be explored without prejudice, starting with the coast, as the coast always has delicious
surprises even for the most demanding palates. Some varieties
along the entire Basque coast—from Bizkaia to Lapurdi—attri-
bute the indirect object marked with the dative case, not to a
canonical dative agreement marker, but instead to a noncanonical
absolutive agreement marker. This way, the corresponding alternative to the already well-known canonical example in (a) would
be the noncanonical and dialectal example in (b):

(123) a. Jonek niri liburua eman di**t**
        Jon.ERG I.DAT book.ABS given to-me-it-has
        "Jon has given me a book"

      b. Jonek niri liburua eman **na**u
        Jon.ERG I.DAT book.ABS given to-me-has

In sentence (a), the indirect object marked with the dative
case *niri* "to me" takes the canonical agreement marker *t*. In sentence (b), on the contrary, the indirect object takes the absolutive agreement marker *na*—both bolded. Moreover, the verbal
form in (b) is bipersonal, which is surprising considering that it
is a sentence with a ditransitive verb (*eman* "to give") and three

arguments (subject, indirect object, and direct object). These kitchens, contrary to what we saw with differential object marking, cook direct objects (something foreseeable in an ergative language such as Basque) and indirect objects (canonically cooked with the dative case) with the absolutive case.

As a result, in many of these varieties where indirect object cooking with the absolutive case is obligatory, bipersonal forms have displaced and substituted tripersonal forms to the point where bipersonal forms are employed with both ditransitive verbs (*eman* "to give") and transitive verbs (*ikusi* "to see").

(124) a. eman nau
　　　　 given to-me-it-has
　　　　 "(S)he has given it to me"

　　　　 b. ikusi nau
　　　　 seen tomehas
　　　　 "(S)he has seen me"

Many dialectologists have considered this phenomenon and the differential object marking phenomenon as the two sides of the same coin: some season (almost) everything with the dative case (with the corresponding tripersonal forms); while others season (almost) everything with the absolutive case (with the foreseeable bipersonal forms). The details justifying distinction between these two phenomena will not be discussed here.

Tasting pintxos while standing at the bar, in good company and possibly with a glass of *txakoli*, the typical sparkling dry white wine from the Basque Country, in hand is different from sitting down to eat a dish with plenty of time, calmly and ceremoniously. In any case, for those foodies without prejudice who want to try this pintxo, it is called *dative displacement*. For a long time, this pintxo had other less technical and more misleading names, such as Louis Lucien Bonaparte's *Idiotisme Marine* (mid-nineteenth century) or Pierre Lafitte's *Solécisme de la Côte* (mid-twentieth century). Readers may judge for themselves.

According to Koldo Zuazo, this is how Basques cook in Lapurdi's southwestern region: starting from Basusarri, Arrangoitze, Arbona, Senpere, Ainhoa, Zugarramurdi, and Urdazubi up to the sea; in Zuraide, Larresoro, and Ezpeleta; in Navarra, Baztan, Bertizarana, and Bortziriak (Five Towns); also in Gipuzkoa between Donostia and Irun; and finally, in Lekeitio, on the Biscayan coast.

Unfortunately, it would be unfair to only try one pintxo when there are so many delicacies atop the counter. In certain varieties (such as those of Pasaia, Oiartzun, or Hondarribia), dative displacement extends to intransitive sentences, and combines with the peculiar selection of the auxiliary verb "to have" instead of the canonical auxiliary verb "to be." The first example (a) is a canonical sentence, and the second one (b) is the noncanonical, dialectal sentence:

(125)   a. Niri lupina gustatzen zait
        I.DAT bass.ABS like to-me
        "I like the bass"

        b. Niri lupina gustatzen nau
        I.DAT bass.ABS like me

Northeastern varieties, on the other hand, omit the dative agreement marker (a) in contexts where the rest of Basque varieties express the overt marker obligatorily (b).

(126)   a. Jonek niri liburua eman dit
        Jon.ERG I.DAT book.ABS given to-me-it-he-has
        "Jon has given me the book"

        b. Jonek niri liburua eman du
        Jon.ERG I.DAT book.ABS given he-has-ut

Furthermore, in Bergara, Antzuola, and Oñati, tripersonal forms containing a third-person indirect object take the noncanonical auxiliary "to be," and the dative agreement marker is attributed to the ergative case (b), instead of taking the canonical auxiliary "to have" and the preposition *ts* preceded by the dative agreement marker (a). We gathered the data presented here in Antzuola:

(127)   a. Zuk hari esan zontsan
           you.ERG he/she.DAT said to-him/her-it-you.have
           "You said it to him/her"

        b. Zuk hari esan jatzun
           you.ERG he/she.DAT said you-to-him/her-it.be
           "You said it to him/her"

As far as I know, there are no systematic theoretical studies about this phenomenon, although it is referenced in the dialectal descriptions of these varieties.

We could go on and on. Anyone who has been to the Basque Country will know first-hand that pintxo-pote bar crawls have a beginning but never an end.

To conclude, readers might wonder whether they need to visit each and every town mentioned to taste all these flavors. They might wonder whether they need to go to Ganbara in Donostia or Xukela in Bilbao. My answer to them is no, not necessarily. Every harbor they visit will have a nice new surprise awaiting them. The key is to explore microgastronomy with an open mind and an open palate. If readers ever come to Algorta, Getxo, they can start, for instance, by trying the grilled foie with toasted nut and raisin bread, apple compote, and caramel at the Old Port's Arrantzale bar. It is about time we name the great female chef behind this pintxo: her name is Idoia Albizu. Readers might be surprised to learn how scarce famous women chefs are in our country, except for Nicolasa Pradera (1870-1959) and her famous restaurant *Casa Nicolasa* that has been open since 1912 on Aldamar Street in Donostia. If we walk past the Old Port's Arrantzale bar headed up Aretxondo Street, we arrive at my forever favorite restaurant: Ereatxu. Ereatxu is a bar run exclusively by women, the Gómez sisters: Marisol, María, and Merche manage the bar, and Marisa and Lourdes manage the kitchen. I invite you to at least try the star pintxo of the house: scrambled eggs with mushrooms. You'll be back for more.

THERE'S NO PLACE LIKE HOME

I opened the chapter with a declaration of principles about the similarities between varieties beyond dialectal differences and about the unification and standardization of Basque, which has allowed the language to achieve a privileged status that languages without a common variety usually do not have. We are absolutely convinced that, years ago, the survival and consolidation of Basque depended on those linguistic kitchen stoves.

Even now, the survival of Basque is not guaranteed. But quite frankly, what we have accomplished throughout the years is impressive, especially given the prejudice and the suffering we have endured.

It might be time to naturally accept that standard Basque obviously has its own social space, which it will hopefully never lose, but that just like any other language, it coexists with its dialects. In fact, standard Basque is a dialect too. This means that some or many of the features of those dialects diverge considerably from the academic norm and what is considered correct, but that these are neither anomalous nor defective varieties for this reason (and neither are the speakers of these varieties). That is a scientific fact.

Regardless of this or other matters that require much more cooking time, I will make language and dialect preservation the pinnacle of this chapter. Basque and Basque dialects are an exponent of linguistic variation, and they can help us better understand the essence of our own language, as well as to appreciate language itself as the essence of human nature.

After all, if such a high number of Basque chefs have made it to the top of international cuisine, it is not only because they are world-acclaimed outstanding professionals, but also because we have so many exceptionally sublime local cuisines. Concerning the author of this book, let me confess that even if I have tried multiple one-, two-, three-starred, and non-Michelin Basque restaurants, there is no better cuisine or chef than those I had during my childhood at home. This chef cooked every weekend, and he might not have won any Michelin stars because he never had a restaurant, but he was the three-time local champion of three specialties (marmitako, pil-pil cod, and ajoarriero cod) that rightfully made him a great Basque chef. Because, quite frankly, there is no place better than home sweet home.

APPENDIX

Some data on the Basque chefs cited in this chapter have been extracted from the text *Claves del éxito de una historia de cooperación entre competidores: El caso de siete grandes cocineros vascos* (*Keys to the Success of a Story of Cooperation among Competitors: The Case of Seven Basque Chefs*), published in Zamudio by Innobasque in 2011.

The Michelin automotive tire guide is already too well known, and we do not want to publicize it even more. The magazine *Restaurant* is responsible for the annual list "The World's 50 Best Restaurants" (also known as the "S. Pellegrino List"— yes, I know I am promoting water), published by William Reed Business Media in England.

For a general summary of Basque dialects, see Zuazo's *Standard Basque and its Dialects*, mentioned in the previous chapter and published by Routledge in 2019. For the current distribution of dialects and their denominations, readers can refer to Zuazo's *Euskalkiak*, published in Basque by Elkar in 2014, as well as *The Dialects of Basque* published by the Center for Basque Studies Press in 2013.

The references to the dialectal geography of the differential object marking in Navarrese Basque were extracted from Koldo Zuazo's article "Nafarroako euskal hizkerak" ("The Basque Varieties of Navarre"). It was published in a volume edited by Iñaki Camino in *Nafarroako hizkerak, Nafarroako Euskal Dialektologiako Jardunaldietako Agiriak* (*The Varieties of Navarre, Proceedings of the Workshops on Navarrese-Basque*

Dialectology) in Bilbao in 1998 by the Basque Summer University (*Udako Euskal Unibertsitatea*) on page 18.

The extract from the conversation between Aitor Iglesias and the speaker from Dima was gathered (and translated) from Beatriz Fernández and Milan Rezac's article "Datibo osagarri bitxiak eta Datiboaren Lekualdatzea: ari nai diyot eta kanta egin nauzu bide-gurutzean" ("Capricious Dative Objects and the Dative Shift"), published in the monographic volume number on Basque syntactic variation *Euskara eta euskarak: aldakortasun sintaktikoa azter-gai (Basque and Basque Dialects: Analyzing Syntactic Variation).* It appeared in the series *Supplements of the Annual Journal of the Basque Studies Seminar (ASJU)*, LII, edited by Beatriz Fernández, Ricardo Etxepare, and Pablo Albizu, and published by the University of the Basque Country (UPV/EHU) on pages 113–149.

I received news of a bar in Bilbao that was awarded an international gastronomic award via a radio show on Euskadi Irratia (literally "Radio Euskadi"), the Basque public radio station that broadcasts entirely in Basque. I am referring to the radio show *Faktoria* hosted by Maite Artola, who interviewed the award-winning chef a few weeks before this book was published in Spanish. Unfortunately, I forgot the name of the bar and the prize, and only the cockscombs—a very peculiar and still relatively unknown specialty—helped me locate the bar Xukela despite it being a challenge. I thank Coli and Txonpa for provid-ing me with the details of the award, and I hope they continue to derive pleasure from the award they won for many years to come.

The term *Idiotisme Marine* (or alternatively *faute de nau*) was coined by Louis Lucien Bonaparte in his work *Le verbe basque en tableaux*, republished in *Opera omnia vasconice (I)* by Euskaltzaindia in Bilbao in 1991, presented on pages 221–242. On the other hand, the term *Solécisme de la Côte* was extracted from Pierre Lafitte's well-known *Grammaire Basque (Navarro-Labourdin Littéraire)* from 1944, republished in Donostia by Elkar in 1979.

Index

About the Author

Beatriz Fernández Fernández is a full professor in the Department of Linguistics and Basque Studies at the University of the Basque Country (UPV/EHU). She received her PhD in 1997 from the same institution and is a corresponding member of the Euskaltzaindia, the official authority on the usages, vocabulary, and grammar of the Basque language. Her research has centered around morphosyntactic variation in Basque, and she has published a variety of articles in international journals such as *Natural Language and Linguistic Theory, Syntax, Linguistic Typology* and *Folia Linguistica* among others. She has also published books on the topic as well as edited compilation volumes for Oxford University Press, John Benjamins, and Brill, among other publishers. The present volume is the English translation of her first book on science intended for the general public. She has one child and currently lives in the Basque Country on the Bay of Biscay.

About the Translator

Eider Etxebarria Zuluaga graduated from the University of Deusto with a bachelor's degree in Modern Languages. She completed her master's degree in Hispanic Linguistics at the University of Illinois at Urbana-Champaign. Currently, she is finishing her doctoral dissertation in Language Acquisition at the University of Illinois at Urbana-Champaign and was awarded the prestigious National Science Foundation Doctoral Dissertation Research Improvement Grant in 2020. She has taught linguistics, Spanish, and Basque at the University of Illinois at Urbana-Champaign. This translation and adaptation project is part of her mission to disseminate Basque language and culture with the aim that English-speakers can inquire more into and come to appreciate our cultural treasure and linguistic heritage.

www.ingramcontent.com/pod-product-compliance
Lightning Source LLC
Chambersburg PA
CBHW070835100426
42813CB00003B/631